MACBETH

A TALE TOLD BY AN IDIOT

The Murderous World of Guilt

MACBETH

A TALE TOLD BY AN IDIOT
The Murderous World of Guilt

KENNETH WAPNICK, Ph.D.

Foundation for A COURSE IN MIRACLES®

Foundation for A Course in Miracles®
41397 Buecking Drive
Temecula, CA 92590
www.facim.org

Printed in China

CONTENTS

INTRODUCTION[1]

Most readers will know that the title, "A Tale Told By An Idiot," is taken from one of Shakespeare's most memorable and extraordinarily powerful speeches. It is from *Macbeth*, Act V, scene v, near the end of the play when Macbeth has learned of his wife's death, most likely by suicide, and is about to go to his own death. We will read the speech in its entirety a bit later.[2]

This book is divided into three parts. I shall first discuss the play and its principal characters. We will see, for example, that Macbeth is Everyman, in the sense that his fate and the decisions he makes represent our own lives. In the second part, I shall discuss Macbeth, not from Shakespeare's point of view, but from the point of view of *A Course in Miracles*, using various readings to depict the progress of Macbeth's life and the choices he made; in particular, his *wrong* choices. In the final part, I shall consider how Macbeth's life could have been different had he listened to the right inner voice instead of the wrong one. I will close by reading a modified version of Macbeth's speech.

The *tale told by an idiot* is really the tale of our lives here, as bodies living in the world. The "idiot" is the ego, and more specifically, it is guilt that tells the tale. As we shall see, guilt is the real hero of the play, as it brings about the tragedy, driving its relentless course throughout. More so than any of Shakespeare's other heroes, Macbeth is clear about the two choices open to him, and just as clear about his conscious choice to kill the king. Thus what gives the play its tragic and heroic grandeur is Macbeth's awareness of what he is doing. He is aware of guilt even before he commits the murder, and it is that guilt that propels him throughout.

Macbeth's tragic flaw, which is *everyone's*, is that he remembered not to laugh at the tiny, mad idea. Indeed, this is the crux of this book. Recall the lines from the text:

---

1. A general introduction to this four-volume series on the great tragedies of Shakespeare appears in the Introduction in Volume I, *King Lear - Love and Be Silent*.
2. A copy may be found in the Appendix.

1

> Into eternity where all is one, there crept a tiny, mad idea, at which the Son of God remembered not to laugh. In his forgetting did it become a serious idea, and possible of both accomplishment and real effects (T-27.VIII.6:2-3).

We looked at the tiny, mad idea of believing we could be separate from God—that we could usurp His place on the throne of creation—and took it seriously. Having done so, we experienced guilt, which not only became a reality but seemed to have very real effects: a *world* of guilt. And that is what we see in *Macbeth*. In this drama we are given a searing and bloody portrait of the world that guilt has wrought. Later, we will look at that wonderfully incisive passage in the text in which Jesus describes our world as the "delusional system of those made mad by guilt" (T-13.in.2:2), and see how Shakespeare depicted that same world in *Macbeth*.

Chapter 1

MACBETH: THE PLAY AND THE CHARACTERS

I would like now to present a summary of the play so that we can place Macbeth's speeches in context and have an understanding of their outer circumstances. Of Shakespeare's quartet of great tragedies, *Macbeth* is the easiest one to read. It is the shortest of the four by almost half, and in terms of construction is probably the finest of Shakespeare's plays. There is hardly a scene that is wasted, and it requires very little editing for performance. *Hamlet,* uncut, is over four hours in length, for example; *Macbeth* is barely two and begins quickly, with a statement of the basic theme that then rapidly unfolds. In Holinshed's *Chronicles (Chronicles of England, Scotland, and Ireland* [1577]), which contains the history of Scotland that Shakespeare used as the basis for the play, Macbeth's reign as king is said to have been 17 years. In the play it is scarcely 17 weeks, so things proceed apace.

The play opens with a gathering of three witches, certainly among Shakespeare's most memorable characters. They appear three times in the play. From a psychological point of view, the witches clearly represent the evil in the human mind. They are actually observed in this play, rather than being presented as hallucinations as Shakespeare does elsewhere. Macbeth sees them; his co-General, Banquo, sees them; and Lady Macbeth, when she is told of them, believes that Macbeth has truly seen them. It is as though when people are ready to choose evil, the witches appear. That is certainly what happens with Macbeth.

The opening lines of the play are spoken by the first witch:

> When shall we three meet again
> In thunder, lightning, or in rain?
>
> $(I,i,1)^3$

Thus the mood of darkness is set that will color the entire play: thunder, lightning, and rain. The atmosphere is murky and ominous, and at the close of this brief scene the witches pronounce the famous lines:

---

3. All Shakespeare quotations are from: *William Shakespeare • The Complete Works •* The Edition of the Shakespeare Head Press, Oxford (New York: Dorset Press, 1988). Line numbers cited refer to the first line quoted.

Fair is foul, and foul is fair;
Hover through the fog and filthy air.

(I,i,10)

The hovering of the foggy, filthy air permeates *Macbeth*, and is the air of guilt. As one would know from studying *A Course in Miracles*, the air of guilt permeates the entire world and the thought system that made the world. This world is not a happy, light-filled place. The love and light that we think are here are really *special* love and *special* light, if you will. Thus we can say, even this early in our discussion, that the value of *Macbeth* as a play, parallel to the Course, is that it defines for us what the *tale told by an idiot* actually is—how the world is the "delusional system of those made mad by guilt."

To continue, Macbeth, a brave and successful general, meets the witches on his return from conquering the foes of Scotland. Both he and Banquo, also a highly-regarded general, are returning to Scotland, having served in the army of King Duncan who, throughout the play, even after he is killed, is referred to as a good, noble, honest man. He is old in years, and is spoken of with the highest regard and respect.

Macbeth is not the incarnation of evil as, for example, Shakespeare's Richard III or Iago in *Othello*. In the early part of the play, Macbeth is seen as good and honorable—brave, courageous, loyal—and so he is treated with respect. When he is greeted by the witches (I,iii,48), they hail him as "Thane of Glamis," "Thane of Cawdor," and "king hereafter." The title "Thane" reflects the play's setting, which takes place in 11th-century Scotland, and is roughly equivalent to "earl" or "baron": people who serve under the king and administer land for him—the governors of certain parts of the country. So Macbeth was Thane of the region called Glamis. There was already a Thane of Cawdor, so Macbeth does not understand why he is hailed by the witches with that title, and why they hail him as king, since Duncan is very much alive.

Macbeth is startled by this greeting, and Banquo notices his friend's reaction. It is obvious that Macbeth has already thought of the idea that he might one day be king. In fact, it is strongly implied that he and his wife have discussed that possibility. Since Duncan's two sons Malcolm and Donalbain are young, and Macbeth is King Duncan's cousin, Macbeth naturally feels that he would be the logical successor to Duncan, who is getting on in years. But when the witches hail him with that appellation, he is taken aback because they seem to have read his mind. From a psychological perspective, we can see that they are really the projection of what is in his mind.

Banquo asks the witches if they would also prophecy for him, although that is not what they had planned to do. Nevertheless, they tell him that while he himself will not be king, his children will be. Later on, in another meeting with the witches, Macbeth has an apparition that shows him the eight kings that will all issue from Banquo's son Fleance.

In the next scene, Duncan appears. He has heard of Macbeth's great successes, and has also heard that the Thane of Cawdor behaved traitorously. Duncan thus orders the traitor executed, and then, without Macbeth knowing it, names him Thane of Cawdor, thus fulfilling one of the witches prophecies. He then greets Macbeth as Thane of Cawdor, lauds him with lavish praise, and then announces to Macbeth's great consternation that Duncan's son Malcolm will be successor to the throne.

Meanwhile, Macbeth has written to Lady Macbeth about the witches' prophecy. Later in the play we learn what Macbeth said to her when she reads part of his letter. (Interestingly, Lady Macbeth does not have a name in the play; she is simply Lady Macbeth.) There are unmistakable indications that the relationship between Macbeth and his wife is quite close. They are a loving couple, sharing openly and honestly with each other, and there is clearly a warmth between them, especially on Macbeth's part.

The plot unfolds rapidly when, after naming Macbeth Thane of Cawdor, Duncan announces that on his way home he will spend the night at Macbeth's castle in Inverness. The scene shifts to the castle, where Lady Macbeth is seen reading her husband's letter, not yet knowing that Duncan will be coming to stay the night. She learns enough, however, to begin to plot the king's overthrow, so that Macbeth will reign in his place. It is evident she is not interested in glory for herself, but that she seeks power and status for her husband. It also is obvious that the idea of being king has been working in Macbeth's mind, and that they had already spoken of this, as I mentioned. However, Lady Macbeth really pushes him now. Even before knowing that Duncan will be visiting, she is musing to herself about the necessity of killing the king, and in her musing she says some words that have become famous, though most people are unaware they come from *Macbeth*. In her musings she is concerned about Macbeth because he is *"too full o' th' milk of human kindness*" (I,v,18). He is too nice a guy, and she thinks he lacks what it would take to actually kill Duncan. She will thus have to push him into doing it. In a chilling speech, she prays to the "*spirits that tend on mortal thoughts*" (I,v,41) to unsex her—to take away her femininity—so she will be like a man and have the courage to bring about Duncan's murder and her husband's success.

Meanwhile, on his way home, Macbeth says something quite important, both in terms of understanding *A Course in Miracles* as well as practicing it. As we will see, it also gives us more insight into him and Lady Macbeth. He is already thinking of killing Duncan so that he can become king, and guilt has begun to build in his mind. He says:

> *Stars, hide your fires;*
> *Let not light see my black and deep desires...*

(I,iv,50)

He is very much aware of his right mind, and thus he is aware that if he listens to its Voice—the Voice that would reflect the light of the stars— it would shine its light on his dark and deep desires and prevent him from killing the king. His prayer is thus to exclude love, light, and his right mind so that he can actually do what the wrong-minded part of him vehemently wishes.

Interestingly, in the next scene Lady Macbeth says the very same thing:

> *Come, thick night,*
> *And pall thee in the dunnest smoke of hell,*

In other words, let the night satiate and fulfill itself with this murky, dark smoke of hell,

> *That my keen knife see not the wound it makes,*
> *Nor heaven peep through the blanket of the dark,*
> *To cry 'Hold, hold!'*

(I,v,51)

We see here an incisive portrait of the split mind. As students of *A Course in Miracles*, we know that the split mind of the Son consists of the right mind, the home of the Holy Spirit and the memory of God, and the ego's wrong mind that wants to usurp God's place on the throne. Finally, there is the decision maker, the part that chooses between the right and wrong minds.

6

At this point in the play we can see that Macbeth represents the decision maker, for he has not yet made up his mind about what he is going to do. The right mind is symbolized by King Duncan, who is seen only as good. In fact, when Macbeth is preparing to kill the king he talks about why he should not do so. Not only is Macbeth Duncan's cousin and serving him well as a general; not only is Duncan staying in his house, and killing him as a guest in his own home would be an even greater sin; but there are Duncan's considerable virtues to think about. He is a good man who does not deserve such a death. Psychologically, therefore, Duncan represents the memory of the Love of God: the great, good, and loving "King" who does not deserve the fate about to befall Him at the hands of the ambitious wrong-minded Son.

Like the witches, Lady Macbeth represents the wrong mind— Macbeth's ego. She is aware of the Voice, the thought of Heaven, which she seeks to exclude; but she is absolutely resolute that Macbeth must kill the king. He proceeds to do so; and as the drama unfolds, Lady Macbeth for a moment believes he has not done it. She says of Duncan: *"Had he not resembled my father as he slept, I had done't"* (II,ii,12). There is some softness in her, but clearly her plea to the spirits to unsex her expresses the decision for the ego she is not going to reverse. She thus represents for Macbeth the wrong-minded pull.

At the end of the 19th century, a respected German scholar named Ludwig Jekels observed that in many of his plays Shakespeare would telescope two characters so that they really became one—two aspects of one self—and the characters of Lady Macbeth and Macbeth were one of his prime examples. Interestingly, Freud, who was always interested in Shakespeare, read Jekels' writings about this, and, as part of a larger paper, discussed his own observations about *Macbeth*, specifically Lady Macbeth, as well as Jekels' theory.

Although he no doubt recognized this, it is interesting that Freud did not make the logical connection in his paper that this shared-character phenomenon is also true of dreams. One way Freud worked with dreams was to show that aspects of the dream were part of the dreamer. Very often the significance of the dream's central figure could be found shared between two characters, which, if put together, would allow the full meaning of the dream to emerge. That certainly can be seen in the characters of Lady Macbeth and Macbeth, who are really two sides of the same coin. We will see as the play goes along that Macbeth's hesitancy and overwhelming sense of guilt are juxtaposed at the beginning with Lady Macbeth's resoluteness and lack of guilt. But once the deed is done, everything shifts. Macbeth becomes the resolute one, without guilt, and Lady Macbeth is consumed with guilt, and eventually destroyed by it. In another example, after Macbeth kills Duncan he hears voices tell him he will no longer be able to sleep. However, at the end of the play it is Lady Macbeth who cannot sleep, as depicted in the famous sleepwalking scene. Again, the two characters are really opposite sides of the same coin, and, as I mentioned, their strong marriage bond reflects that they are of one mind, trading off the guilt.

To return to the play, Macbeth is on his way home to Inverness, where Duncan is preparing to spend the night. Lady Macbeth is already hatching the plot, and even before Macbeth and Duncan arrive, an attendant informs Lady Macbeth that Duncan is spending the night. She quickly works everything out, so when Macbeth returns she presents him with the plan: There will be two guards posted at the door outside the room where Duncan will be sleeping. She will drug the guards so they fall asleep. Macbeth will kill the king and place his daggers on the guards, so they will be accused of the assassination. She presents this plan to Macbeth, who hesitates for the reasons I have discussed. In responding he says:

> *But in these cases*
> *We still have judgment here; that we but teach*
> *Bloody instructions, which, being taught, return*
> *To plague th'inventor...*

(I,vii,7)

Later we will look at a passage in *A Course in Miracles* directly parallel to this, where Jesus talks about how, when we project, we believe our projections will creep back in. That is what Macbeth is saying here. He is aware that once he embarks on this life of murder, it will never end, a premonition of his own death, perhaps. In fact, at the end of the play he, too, is murdered. Again:

> *that we but teach*
> *Bloody instructions, which, being taught, return*
> *To plague th'inventor...*

This also brings to mind a well-known line from the gospels where Jesus tells Peter that all those who live by the sword shall die by the sword (Matthew 26:52).

We thus see how at the beginning Macbeth was becoming aware of the effects of his choice. This, however, did not deter him from his decision to proceed with the murder. Before that, Lady Macbeth used every type of persuasion, basically accusing Macbeth of not being manly if he did not murder Duncan, and she implied that she will henceforth base her love for him on whether or not he acts, although I do not think Macbeth would have taken that threat seriously. Nor do I think any of his wife's arguments would have swayed Macbeth; he was already in the grip of his dark side. Therein lay his guilt, which is what makes Macbeth's everyone's story. He is aware that what he is doing is wrong. Undoubtedly he is aware—once he embarks on a life of murder, usurpation, and sin—that guilt will drive him to live in a world of murder in which he will never be safe, as we shall see presently.

Let us read some other famous lines that convey this guilt. Just before he kills Duncan, Macbeth hallucinates a dagger and says:

> *Is this a dagger which I see before me,*
> *The handle toward my hand? Come, let me clutch thee:–*
> *I have thee not, and yet I see thee still.*
> *Art thou not, fatal vision, sensible*
> *To feeling as to sight? or art thou but*
> *A dagger of the mind, a false creation,*
> *Proceeding from the heat-oppressed brain?*
>
> (II,i,33)

There is no dagger. Macbeth is clearly projecting an hallucinatory image of what he is about to do, his guilt now having become a disturbing force. Following this experience, he, undeterred by guilt, proceeds to kill Duncan.

Perhaps some of you saw the *Macbeth* film made over 30 years ago by Roman Polanski. Sharon Tate was Polanski's wife, and he produced the film shortly after she had been murdered by the Charles Manson group. It was an extremely bloody movie, and in a sense, making the film was a catharsis for Polanksi. In the film, Duncan's murder, which is offstage in Shakespeare's original, happens on camera. Macbeth is shown hesitating as he is about to commit the act. It is only when Duncan suddenly arouses from his sleep, opens his eyes and sees Macbeth, that our hero is impelled to complete the murderous act. I do not think that was what Shakespeare had in mind. Macbeth did not need to have Duncan see him to be pushed over the precipice. Macbeth was already determined, and inexorably headed in that direction, which is why the witches appeared to him.

Macbeth thus kills Duncan and is overwhelmed with guilt. Shortly afterwards he says the lines alluded to above:

> *Methought I heard a voice cry 'Sleep no more!*
> *Macbeth does murder sleep,'–the innocent sleep,*
> *Sleep that knits up the ravell'd sleeve of care...*

> (II,ii,34)

Then he continues a bit later:

> *Still it cried "Sleep no more!" to all the house:*
> *'Glamis* [recall that Macbeth was the Thane of Glamis] *hath*
> *murder'd sleep, and therefore Cawdor*
> *Shall sleep no more,–Macbeth shall sleep no more!'*

> (II,ii,40)

Macbeth is haunted by guilt over what he has done; and again, what makes Macbeth such a tragically heroic figure, if not an evil one, is that he is fully aware of what is going on. He was aware of the guilt before he committed the murder, no doubt while he was killing Duncan, and is overwhelmed with it afterwards. This awareness, however, does not stop him. That is the tragedy.

He comes to Lady Macbeth with the daggers, saying, "*I have done the deed*" (II,ii,14), and she is furious because he did not follow the plan, which was to place the daggers on the two sleeping guards, not to keep them. Macbeth obviously does not want to do that, and will not do it. His guilt gives the compelling reason:

> *I'll go no more:*
> *I am afraid to think what I have done;*
> *Look on't again I dare not.*

> (II,ii,49)

Many of you will remember that when I outline the myth of the ego in my lectures, I stress the strategic importance to the ego of the Son being convinced he has committed a terrible sin against God. The Son would then be so overwhelmed with guilt that he would never look at it, forever turning away from it. It is this fear of looking at our guilt that drives us to project it out, making up a world that becomes our hiding place so that we never have to look at the guilt in our minds. Like

Macbeth, we do not want to see what we have done. Macbeth thus utters these words for all of us:

> *I am afraid to think what I have done;*
> *Look on't again I dare not.*

He will not look at it, so Lady Macbeth basically says: "All right, I shall take care of it. After all, it is just a little blood and it will wash clean." She takes the daggers, smears them with Duncan's blood (this is not seen on stage, but is alluded to), and places them on the two sleeping guards. What Macbeth could not complete she does. Again, they act as a team. As I mentioned, they not only share complicity in the murder, but the guilt as well.

Macbeth then says:

> *Had I but died an hour before this chance,*
> *I had lived a blessed time;* [he is already regretting what he has
>   done] *for, from this instant,*
> *There's nothing serious in mortality:* [death is nothing; life is
>   nothing]
> *All is but toys: renown and grace is dead;*
> *The wine of life is drawn, and the mere lees*
> *Is left this vault to brag of.*

(II,iii,92)

"*Lees*" refers to the dregs of the wine, the left-over sediment. Macbeth is saying that what is left now is worth nothing, for the wine of life is gone: "*The wine of life is drawn*"—it is now consumed—"*and the mere lees is left this vault to brag of.*" All that remains is a meaninglessness life because of what I have done. If you think of this within an ontological context, Shakespeare is saying through his protagonist that once the deed of killing the king is done—the "deed" symbolizing our killing of God—everything else is worthless. This becomes the theme of the "*tale told by an idiot*" speech.

Macbeth is aware, from this point on, that he will never be safe. The more he kills, the greater is his guilt, and the greater still is his belief that he will be attacked. It is a classic expression of guilt deserving punishment. The more we have attack thoughts and the angrier we become, no matter how much we may try to justify our rage, the guilt keeps intensifying; our attack thoughts are reminiscent of the original attack thought against God. The guilt becomes so horrendous and blinding that all we can do is deny it, project it, and then believe that everyone is seeking to kill us as punishment for our secret sin of murder. Thus we feel justified to kill everyone else first, and so it is that Macbeth embarks on a career of murder and cruelty. His life has now been so cheapened by what he has done that murder is easy, and he no longer hesitates. He crossed the line, having made an irrevocable decision for the ego rather than the Holy Spirit. From this point on, everything is guilt, hate, attack, murder, defense—which is what Macbeth means when he says:

> *To be thus is nothing;* [to be the king now is nothing]
> *But to be safely thus.*
>
> (III,i,47)

Ah, that is something else. Hamlet would have said: *"To be safely thus. Ay, there's the rub"* (*Hamlet*, III,i,65). Macbeth will nevermore be safe.

Duncan's murder is discovered, but Macbeth feigns total ignorance, as well as anger and indignation at the two guards, as it seems obvious they are the murderers. He quickly dispatches them with his dagger before they have the opportunity to protest their innocence. Life is now very cheap for Macbeth, and he keeps on killing. Duncan's two sons Malcolm and Donalbain, who were also staying overnight in the castle, quickly realize their lives are at risk and flee—Malcolm to England and Donalbain to Ireland. Macbeth uses their flight to arouse suspicion about them: "You know, maybe it wasn't the guards. Maybe I acted too hastily. It was probably Malcolm and Donalbain. They killed their father so Malcolm would be king." His strategy works, and Malcolm and Donalbain are now suspected of the crime. Macbeth is recognized as the likely successor and is very quickly crowned king, which is the poignancy of his words: *"To be thus is nothing; but to be safely thus—."* That is the problem. His good friend and co-General Banquo is also at the castle, and Banquo, who is no fool, begins to realize that something is very rotten in the state of Scotland. Macbeth senses his friend's distrust and will quickly seize the opportunity to claim his next victim. He says:

> *Our fears in Banquo*
> *Stick deep; and in his royalty of nature* [namely, that his sons will
>   be kings]
> *Reigns that which would be fear'd...*
>
> (III,i,48)

Macbeth, who still has not lost his ability to reflect on what he is doing, says a bit later to his wife:

We have scotcht the snake, not kill'd it...

(III,ii,13)

We have rendered the snake harmless and I am now king, but I have not killed it. I am thus still at risk and will never be safe:

She'll close, [the snake will close and be herself]; whilst our poor malice
Remains in danger of her former tooth.

(III,ii,14)

In other words, the malice is still there: hate will breed hate; malice will breed malice; murder will breed murder, and I will nevermore be safe. In the language borrowed from *A Course in Miracles*, Macbeth could have said: "The hate I projected out will creep back in, and I will remain in danger."

But let the frame of things disjoint, both the worlds suffer,
Ere we will eat our meal in fear, and sleep
In the affliction of these terrible dreams
That shake us nightly: better be with the dead,
Whom we, to gain our peace, have sent to peace,
Than on the torture of the mind to lie
In restless ecstasy.

(III,ii,16)

Macbeth is now gripped by guilt, but it does not restrain him in any way. To the contrary—it impels him to act in guilt-inducing and guilt-reinforcing ways.

Another indication of Macbeth's awareness comes at the end of this scene when he says:

Things bad begun make strong themselves by ill...

(III,ii,54)

A self-reinforcing cycle has been set in motion, making itself strong by further ill; by further attack and sin. Thus is Macbeth in the grips of this dangerously powerful ego cycle of guilt-attack-defense-guilt-attack. From within that cycle there is no way out.

Rather quickly now Macbeth arranges with two murderers to have Banquo killed, along with his son Fleance. Macbeth reasons: "If

Banquo is dead, he cannot have any more children; and if his son Fleance is dead, I am forevermore safe!" To make sure the deed is done, Macbeth even dispatches a third murderer. But they fail to complete their task. Banquo is killed, but the son escapes. (I have been unable to find any information on where Fleance went—perhaps to England, too.)

A great feast had been scheduled at which Banquo, among others, would be honored as a victorious general. Banquo of course does not show up, but his ghost apparently does—at least to Macbeth's hallucinating eyes. Unlike the ghost of Hamlet's father, no one else sees Banquo's ghost. A guilt-ridden Macbeth addresses the ghost: "Do not shake your gory locks at me; I did not do it." Strictly speaking he did not; the appointed murderers committed the deed. Lady Macbeth, who still has her wits about her, covers for her husband and says to the people, in effect:, "You know, Macbeth is like this. Every once in awhile he gets carried away by emotion, becomes a bit crazed and faints." Then she herself faints. The guests are dismissed and everyone now is aware that something is terribly wrong.

Shakespeare does not enumerate the long list of cruelties, but it is obvious from what people say that Macbeth has killed anyone he suspected of not being in his camp. Macduff, a nobleman and soldier, concludes that Macbeth must be Duncan's killer and thus realizes he will be next. He thus also flees to England, where he joins with Malcolm, son of Duncan, and they prevail upon King Siward of England to help them. They gather an army to return and attack Macbeth. Macbeth hears about it, and for no reason arranges to have Lady Macduff and her small children killed. Those murders serve no purpose, since Macduff is not around. They simply reflect Macbeth's relentless cruelty and vengeance that motivate him to have the mother and her children brutally killed.

Consequent upon his decision to kill Duncan, Macbeth has become more and more estranged from everyone. What drove the original choice to separate from Duncan, first betraying him in his mind and then actually slaying him, now permeates everything. At this point Lady Macbeth has basically disappeared and is not seen again until the very end of the play. It is obvious, though, that her relationship with her husband has become estranged. Macbeth no longer counsels with her; he kills Banquo without informing her, as he does Lady Macduff and the children. Indeed, he now does everything without informing her, whereas previously everything was done in tandem. He is completely alienated from the one person he loved and trusted, and has separated himself from everyone else. Needless to say, alienating ourselves from everyone epitomizes the life of the ego.

In the final act, Lady Macbeth reappears. She has gone mad. Not even her physician can do anything for her. Macbeth at one point speaks to him, having become impatient at his inability to help his wife, but it is obvious Macbeth no longer has feelings for her. She now spends her time trying to wash Duncan's blood from her hands, whereas earlier in the play she had cavalierly dismissed the spilled blood, saying that she would wash it off and no one would ever know. But in her madness the blood remains, and we witness the famous sleepwalking scene. Later I will point out a number of the common elements in Lady Macbeth's speech and a passage in the manual based directly on her words. Here are a few excerpts from the scene:

> *Out, damned spot! Out, I say!–One, two; why, then,'tis time to do't.–*
> *Hell is murky!–Fie, my lord, fie! A soldier, and afeard?* [She relives the killing of Duncan and makes fun of her husband.] *What need we fear who knows it, when none can call our power to account?...*
>
> (V,i,35)

Virtually every tyrant, dictator, and president, get into this. They become obsessed with the arguments of power and say to themselves: "Why do we have to be afraid? We have the power. And if someone challenges us, we will simply dispense with them."

Then come these bone-chilling lines:

> *Yet who would have thought the old man to have had so much blood in him?*
>
> (V,i,39)

She is now obsessed with the blood. In fact, the symbol of blood permeates the entire play. Here, of course, blood is the symbol of her and her husband's sin.

She now reflects on Lady Macduff's murder, chilling in its pedestrian quality:

> *The thane of Fife had a wife; where is she now?–What, will these hands ne'er be clean?*
>
> (V,i,42)

She continues washing her hands, but she cannot remove the stains of blood and says:

> *Here's the smell of the blood still: all the perfumes of Arabia will not sweeten this little hand.*
>
> (V,i,50)

The stench of her sin is so great there is no way she can escape it. And, as I mentioned earlier, she feels the guilt that Macbeth no longer consciously feels. He simply continues without restraint, killing wantonly with absolute callousness and cruelty.

Lady Macbeth says to herself:

> *Wash your hands, put on your nightgown; look not so pale:– I tell you yet again, Banquo's buried; He cannot come out on's grave.*
>
> (V,i,61)

Remember, Macbeth had seen Banquo's ghost. Here Lady Macbeth is saying to him, why are you making all this up? He is dead. And then she says:

> *To bed, to bed; there's knocking at the gate: ...*

This is a reference to the famous drunken-porter scene. Earlier in the play, right after Macbeth killed Duncan, there was a knock on the door. It was late at night and a porter was supposed to have been standing at the gate. He obviously was very drunk, and when he heard knocking at the gate, in his intoxicated state he thought it was a knocking at the gates of hell, which was most appropriate in terms of what had just gone on. Thus she says:

> *there's knocking at the gate: come, come, come, come, give me your hand: what's done cannot be undone: ...*
>
> (V,i,65)

Those lines are also the basis for a phrase in the section of the manual I just referred to: "for what was done cannot be done without" (M-17.7:12). Once the decision to kill was made, once the belief in sin was accorded reality, once guilt arises, nothing can ever change unless the basic decision for guilt is undone. Once we embark on the ego thought system, there is no way out from within that system. That is what Jesus means when he says in *A Course in Miracles* that the ego's thought system is fool-proof (T-5.VI.10:6).

"What's done cannot be undone." Once we believe we are separated and are here in bodily form, we are doomed by the very fact that we believe we are here; doomed by the very thought system that gives seeming life to us. We are doomed to continually repeat the pattern of guilt that got us here in the world. Indeed, guilt is what made the world. Our fearful belief that God will destroy us if we are not careful is echoed in the play with Banquo's ghost rising from the grave to haunt Macbeth's guilt. In those terms, we fear that we, too, will see daggers in front of us and not be able to escape the wrath of God as punishment for our sin and guilt. The only thing we can do now is deny guilt's presence, project it out, and see evil all around us, allowing us to feel justified in killing it. On a behavioral level, almost none of us would behave as did Macbeth—acting out his guilt by killing everyone he even suspected of being an enemy or traitor. But we all engage in that life of murder every instant we hold separating thoughts about anyone. Every thought of specialness is, in fact, a thought of murder.

Most students will remember a line from *A Course in Miracles* that could just as well have been written by Shakespeare: "What is not love is murder" (T-23.IV.1:10). Special love—a love built on separation—is clearly not the Love of Heaven, which is a Thought of perfect Oneness. This means that every expression of love in this world, if it is exclusively between two people, or among a select group of people that excludes others, is murderous. Love that expresses neediness and demand our needs be met by some special other is murderous at heart. Thus, while none of us would stoop to Macbeth's level of wanton killing, we nonetheless continually act out his murderousness in our minds. We do not murder in deed, but in thought. That is why Macbeth is all of us.

In the sleepwalking scene Lady Macbeth is obviously consumed by guilt. She is then seen no more, and when we next hear of her, it is when the doctor informs Macbeth of her death. It is never clearly stated that she has taken her own life, but that is the unmistakable implication. There is no indication that she was murdered or died of natural causes. Since the ego thought system tells us that the ultimate goal of guilt is death, the guilt-ridden Lady Macbeth's apparent suicide is consistent with that thought system.

Macbeth is unmoved by this news. When he hears about his wife's death, all he can say is:

She should have died hereafter;
There would have been a time for such a word.

(V,v,16)

In other words, she died much too early; she should have lived a longer life. Macbeth next commences the *"Tomorrow, and tomorrow, and tomorrow"* speech, which we will discuss in a moment.

Before Lady Macbeth's sleepwalking drama, Macbeth had summoned the three witches because he had become preoccupied with recent events, and was obviously concerned about his own death. He is well aware that those who live by the sword die by the sword, so he summons the witches for a prophecy, and demands that they tell him what is going to happen. In turn, they summon apparitions that speak to Macbeth, and they tell him seemingly contradictory things. For instance, they say he should be afraid of Macduff, but then he does not have to worry for he need only be afraid of a man who is not born of a woman. Since Macbeth does not know of anyone who is not born of a woman, he feels secure. He is also told that he does not have to worry until Birnam Wood comes to Dunsinane, which is the area where his castle is located. Birnam Wood is a forest not very far away, but far enough, and obviously there is no way a forest is going to pick itself up and self-transport to the castle; so Macbeth again thinks he is fine and has nothing to worry about.

He is pondering all this in his mind when he is then told of Lady Macbeth's death, whereupon he makes the wonderfully evocative speech. Following this soliloquy, a messenger tells Macbeth, in horror, to look outside: Birnam Wood is coming to Dunsinane (V,v,28). What has happened is that Malcolm and Macduff have joined forces with King Siward of England, and in order for their army to approach Macbeth's forces without being detected, they have cut branches from the trees of Birnam Wood to use as camouflage, holding them in front so they would not be seen. Thus Birnam Wood had indeed come to Dunsinane!

Macbeth is shaken, but the second prophecy has not yet been fulfilled. He confronts King Siward's younger son, who, having identified Macbeth as the murderous tyrant, bravely takes him on in battle. The young man is no match for Macbeth, however, who kills him just as he did so many others. Finally, he is confronted by Macduff, who is filled with rage and lusting for vengeance for his slain family. He wants

Macbeth's head, and in fact had promised Malcolm he would return with it. The two soldiers stand face to face, and Macbeth boasts to Macduff that he cannot hurt him; he can be hurt only by someone who is not born of a woman. Macduff then informs him, speaking of himself in the third person:

> *Macduff was from his mother's womb*
> *Untimely ript.*

(V,vii,15)

In other words, he was born via Cesarean section and did not go through the birth canal. Therefore, technically, he was not born of a woman. This does not deter Macbeth, however. Hellbent on murder, and obviously hellbent on his own death as expiation for his guilt, he utters the famous words:

> *lay on, Macduff;*
> *And damn'd be him that first cries "Hold, enough!"*

(V,viii,33)

They fight (off stage), and Macduff kills him, returning with Macbeth's head on a pole, as promised. Malcolm now is to be crowned king as the play ends.

In his movie, Polanski—and I am not particularly recommending his very bloody and not at all pleasant film—did a brilliant thing. He included something that was not from Shakespeare, though I think it was inspired by Jesus. At the movie's close, Polanski has Donalbain— the younger son whose royal aspirations were passed over in favor of Malcolm—confront the three witches as he is on the road. The point is quite clear: evil goes on. If we understand that the witches appear only when they are summoned by the unconscious ego, we realize that Donalbain is going to embark on the same hellish road as did Macbeth. The ego's circle of guilt and hate is unending. But in Shakespeare's play, that is not how it ends. When Macbeth is killed, Malcolm, a good man and supported by Macduff, is hailed King of Scotland.

Let us now read Macbeth's famous soliloquy. In the copy included in the Appendix, I titled it "Song of Guilt," and it is accompanied by the "Song of Innocence," a right-minded recasting of this speech, which I shall read as a closing. Here is Macbeth:

To-morrow, and to-morrow, and to-morrow,
Creeps in this petty pace from day to day,
To the last syllable of recorded time;
And all our yesterdays have lighted fools
The way to dusty death. Out, out, brief candle!
Life's but a walking shadow; a poor player,
That struts and frets his hour upon the stage,
And then is heard no more: it is a tale
Told by an idiot, full of sound and fury,
Signifying nothing.

(V,v,18)

That is a magnificent rendering of the world of guilt, and of the thought system from which it emanates. I have spoken a great deal in my writings and classes about how this ego thought system of sin-guilt-fear, when projected from the mind, gives rise to linear time: past-present-future. We believe we have sinned in the past; in what we think of as the present we experience guilt—an overwhelming sense of self-hatred; finally, we project our guilt into a fearful future where punishment awaits us for our past sins. That is what Macbeth expresses in this speech.

"Tomorrow, and tomorrow, and tomorrow"—day in and day out—we creep in this petty pace, to the very end: *"the last syllable of recorded time."* The very end is death: *"And all our yesterdays have lighted fools the way to dusty death."* Anyone who thinks that there is anything going on here in this world is a fool. Anyone who thinks there is any hope, love, or light in this world is a fool. The *"brief candle"* that Macbeth seeks to extinguish is physical life, and he clearly foresees his own death: *"Out, out, brief candle! Life's but a walking shadow."* In the context of the ego thought system described in *A Course in Miracles*, life in the body is a shadow—literally a shadow—of the thought of guilt in our minds. What we really experience here is a shadow acting out a drama that ends in death; thus our body *"struts and frets his hour upon the stage and then is heard no more."*

It is all a *"tale told by an idiot, full of sound and fury."* We think this world is of immense importance, and certainly Macbeth's world was of immense importance to him. He was king. There were many sounds of battle, sounds of glory, and certainly sounds of fury. But they all came to naught and signified nothing. The world of time and space—birth, life, and death—is but a shadow of the thought of guilt in our minds, the ultimate expression of which is death. When we separated from the Everything that is God—true life—the ultimate expression of our guilt became the nothingness of death. The world is a shadow of that original thought of separation, which is nothing and so the world is nothing. In spite of the ego's cacophony—the seeming sounds of glory, pleasure, and happiness in this world—they are all but *"sound and fury, signifying nothing."*

In a different context, when King Lear says *"Nothing will come of nothing"* (*King Lear*, I,i,90), he is expressing a similar idea. If you say nothing, nothing will come of it. In essence, he was telling his daughter Cordelia: "If you say nothing and are silent, then you will get nothing from me and will be cast out of my kingdom." In a sense, that is what the ego tells us, and the ego's words are nothing and the sound of nothing. Being nothing, the ego's effect is nothing as well.

Since the birth of the ego is consequent upon the death of God, death would have to be our reality within the dream of separation, and would thus permeate our entire lives. The projection of the ego thought system results in a world of death, wherein everything dies, or somehow comes to an end. We try to cover over the horror of life here in this world—which the play *Macbeth* depicts in an almost ghoulish way—and make it into something pretty. We take murder and try to justify it. To Macbeth's credit, he never tried to justify what he was doing. For example, his drive for power he says is a

> *Vaulting ambition, which o'erleaps itself,*
> *And falls on th'other.*

(I,vii,27).

Macbeth's ambition goes beyond itself and falls on another: Duncan. He does not care, for he is driven. He does not try to justify it, nor does he call it freedom, democracy, salvation, God, or love. He is quite clear that it is murder. This is what gives him a certain grandeur, even though he ends up a monster. He was not always like that; and we were not always the way we are: obsessed with specialness. There is a part of our minds that is a doorway back home. There is a part of our minds that still holds the memory of love and light, like a forgotten song (T-21.I), but we keep it buried, as did Macbeth.

Again, to our hero's credit, he never tried to justify his turning away from love. We, on the other hand, are not quite as noble as he, for we continually try to justify our hate and murderousness, our specialness

21

and grandiosity. We seek to justify our attempts to be number one, to be king, to be the most loved, the most highly approved of, the center of attention. We strive always to justify our egos. Of course, such rationalizations delay our inevitable confrontation with guilt. Macbeth was not able to do that, and that is why he became overwhelmed by it, caught up in a life of such chilling cruelty that he never rests or truly sleeps again. Always afraid, he has to keep killing to protect himself. We, on the other hand, purchase momentary satisfaction. It never lasts very long, but we are able to place a veil over our inner life and motivations so that we have moments of peace, comfort, pleasure, joy, and happiness. We magically arrange our worlds to convince ourselves that this passing satisfaction and substitute for love will last—that it is real and true. We never want to look at the shadowy world of guilt and fear that lies underneath, and which is revealed to us in Macbeth's final soliloquy.

The very fact that we are here in a body testifies to our desire to kill the King Duncans of the world. We want to kill the authorities, usurp their role and sit on their throne; and we do not care who pays the price. Our guilt over this is horrendous! Neither are there words strong enough to express the depths of such self-hatred. But just as Macbeth knew, we, too, know there is a better way. However, our guilt escalates to such gargantuan proportions that all we can do is drive it underground and believe in the efficacy of magic to save us.

Macbeth drove his guilt underground, too, and it came out as a life of raw, murderous cruelty. We drive it underground, but with very few exceptions it comes out as special love in our world. Even when we kill—even when those in power kill—we try to justify it. We should give Saddam Hussein a little credit for not trying to justify the cruelties he perpetrated. At least he was honest about what he was doing. In no way does that excuse the cruelty, but at least he was honest enough not to lie to himself and call it by a pretty name.

When we look at Macbeth, we should take that same nobility of awareness and apply it to ourselves by not trying to label what we do with a name other than what it is: hate, murder, usurpation, and the ambition to be on top, to be first in someone's attention, affection, and love. We want to be number one, whether it is to have the most power in the world, the most money, the most lovers, the best children, the best job, or the best body. Whatever it is, we want to be first. And we can strive to be first on the flip side, too: the world's worst tyrant; its greatest victim, having suffered the most pain and misery, or being the most utterly abandoned. The ego just wants more. It does not matter more of what. It could be more nobility as king, or more ignobility as the lowliest serf—being on the top or bottom—as long as you are the best and the most of what you are, even if means being the best of the worst. All the ego cares about is our worshipping idols at its altar of specialness. As Jesus explains in the section called "The Anti-Christ," the ego wants "more than everything."

> Each worshipper of idols harbors hope his special deities will give him more than other men possess. It must be more. It does not really matter more of what; more beauty, more intelligence, more wealth, or even more affliction and more pain. But more of something is an idol for (T-29.VIII.8:6-9).

Honesty lies in looking at that motivation, and what will get you headed in the right direction is realizing that if you are here in a body, then you must have made the same choice as Macbeth. That is why *Macbeth* is such a compelling play, and why he is such a compelling character. Macbeth is the least likable of Shakespeare's great tragic heroes—Hamlet, Othello, Lear, and himself—and this makes sense because he is Everyone, and he knew about guilt and forgiveness, just as we do. Jesus makes the point repeatedly in *A Course in Miracles* that we know we have a wrong and right mind, and have a choice between them. We do not like to admit this, however, because the guilt over our choosing the ego is too great.

Many of you have read *A Course in Miracles* many times, over many years, and you know. You cannot say any more that you do not understand, or that you do not know you have a choice. Although it is not in the published Course in these literal words, near the end of the scribing of the text, Jesus essentially told Helen, "You cannot say you do not understand this. I have explained it all to you, and you have written it down." So, like Helen, we know all this. The ego thought system has been explained to us; and still we make the wrong choice, even though we clearly know what we are doing, as did Macbeth.

Again, the point here is that, like Macbeth, we understand the consequences of our ego choices. The main thrust of *A Course in Miracles* is to make it clear to us that we know exactly what we are doing—that whenever we choose to get angry, pick a fight, or indulge our specialness, we are "choosing to kill King Duncan" and attempting to get away with it. We take the daggers and smear them with the blood of our guilt; then we put them on innocent people, killing them so that no one will know the truth. We want to commit the crime. We want to kill the king and blame others for the sin. The problem is that the self-blame remains in our minds. As Macbeth says: "*We have scotcht the snake, not kill'd it*" (III,ii,13). We have what we want, but the guilt has not left: I know I am the one who did it, and that I actively chose to do so. Jesus tries to have us understand in his Course that we know we are choosing to kill the king each and every time we choose anger or any aspect of special-ness, or make a judgment or comparison:

> If you perceived the special relationship as a triumph over God, would you want it? (T-16.V.10:1)

We will not escape the burden of guilt unless we finally look at it from a right mind-minded perspective.

As long as our guilt remains, its effects will be devastating, all the more since we do not recognize the source of our devastation. Some-times our experience is that we have been "blind-sided"—apparently victimized by something we did not see coming. We suddenly find our-selves enraged, fearful, impatient, or anxious; or we wake up depressed and are not really sure why—it all seems to come out of nowhere. The explanation remains the same, however. The underlying cause of all distress is our decision to be separate; to push Jesus or the Holy Spirit away, and follow the ego instead. The effect of that decision is anger, fear, pain, suffering, and aggravation—the ego attacks we experience daily.

The ego made time and space to be a gap between *cause*, the deci-sion for guilt we make in our minds, and *effect*, the world. There is thus this huge chasm between cause and effect—cosmically as well as indi-vidually. The purpose of *A Course in Miracles* is to teach us to bring the effect back to the cause, that we may be aware that the choice for wrong-mindedness will inevitably lead to painful consequences. Therefore, if we continue to make the choice for the ego, it is because we do not care about the consequences. We want what we want when we want it! I want to be king, and if someone is in the way, that is too bad. However, if we make that choice with open eyes, as Macbeth did, and realize that there are going to be undesirable consequences, in the end we will overcome our attitude of *wanting what we want when we want it*, and be motivated to make the wrong-minded choice less and less often.

In this context we can restate the principle, *ideas leave not their source*, as *effects leave not their cause*. The idea is an *effect* and the source is the mind, which is *cause*. The more we shrink the gap between choosing wrong-mindedness—the *cause*—and experiencing the negative consequences of that choice—the *effect*—the easier it becomes to refrain from that choice.

From another point of view, the experience of being blind-sided affords us the opportunity of evading responsibility for our condition in the world and putting on the face of innocence, another major chapter in the ego's mind-training manual. "It is not my fault" then becomes our favorite song, unaware that it is the dirge of an ill-intentioned composer, dedicated to obliterating the power of the mind from our awareness. The ego will always attempt to associate our decisions with guilt, which then forces us to think anxiously: "I cannot look at this." Thus Macbeth said to Lady Macbeth, in effect: "I am not going back in there; I do not want to see what I have done." We do the same, which is why we made up a world with other figures in it: the blood will be on their hands, not our own. We do not want to look and we do not want the responsibility of having chosen. The guilt we associate with our decision to be with the ego is our problem, which is why I said earlier that *Macbeth* is a play about guilt. This theme can be found throughout Shakespeare, but in *Macbeth* it is front and center, the reason for its instructiveness.

As I have stated, we will not escape the burden of guilt unless we finally look at it from our right minds. Macbeth arranged his inner life so that he could no longer hear another Voice. He did not summon the Holy Spirit; he summoned the voice of the witches and listened to the voice of his wife. Even though the Voice for God was present in his mind, he chose not to listen. Recall that both he and Lady Macbeth— two sides of the same ego coin—shared the plea that the stars of Heaven hide their fires so that the light will not shine on their dark thoughts (I,iv,50). We made up a world for that very reason: so that the light of Heaven in our minds would not shine on our "secret sins and hidden hates" (T-31.VIII.9:2), thereby undoing them and healing our minds. The darkest of these thoughts is our selfishly wanting what we want, no matter who pays the price. The ego sees to it that there will always be people to pay the price—sleeping guards drugged by another part of our minds so that we have someone to blame; someone upon whom to put the bloody daggers so they will be seen as the evil perpetrators and therefore the ones to be punished. But the lesson of the play is that you can never escape your guilt.

Once again, this is a play about guilt, the end product of which is the *"tale told by an idiot, full of sound and fury, signifying nothing."* Even when you get what you thought you wanted, it does not last. You secure your individual existence and sit on the throne of your life, but it does not last because your guilt will demand that someone take it from you. The ego's fourth law of chaos is that "you have what you have taken" (T-23.II.9). Macbeth had the throne, but he had it because he *took* it from the king. In order for us to exist, we had to take our throne from God. Once you have wrested what you want from another, you project the guilt from that theft and then believe that others will take from you what you secretly believed you stole from them. "You have what you have taken" means that someone else does not have it because you have it. So now you begin to suspect that everyone is trying to get back what you took. The more suspicious and guilty you are, the more you have to attack others and kill them, whether physically, as did Macbeth, or psychologically through specialness.

This cycle of attack, guilt, and defense keeps everything in this world going. Eventually it ends up as a self-fulfilling prophecy, as happened with Macbeth, where people actually did plot against him because he killed, or tried to kill, everyone. Of course, the ego likes that even better, because when we can see that people are really out to get us, then we do not have to make it up. We do not have to have a paranoid hallucination, or a delusional system where we are made mad by guilt. Thus do our egos welcome the attacks of others. But it does not matter whether they actually attack or not; we believe they will.

What makes *Macbeth* a disturbing play, to make this point one more time, is that it is everyone's play. It brings the underground in human affairs to the surface. As I have said, the blood that is spilled and the murky atmosphere throughout depicts the true nature of our lives here. We try to cover over this truth and make everything look pretty. We really believe we can wash the blood off our hands and rid our bodies of the stench of death, the awful odor of murder. But we cannot, because our very lives derive from murder, and the lungs that inhale oxygen to keep us going also breathe in the guilt of our sin. Murder is how we got here and how our lives here are sustained.

We all experience needs here. If you do not breathe for fifteen or twenty seconds, you are going to feel very uncomfortable. If you do not eat for forty-eight hours, you are going to get very uncomfortable; and for some people it only takes two hours. That is how we know we are not in Heaven. There are no needs in Heaven, physical or psychological If we experience need—as we all do—obviously we cannot be in Heaven. If we are not in Heaven, how did we get *here*? Only through the mad thought that we destroyed Heaven and made our own world as replacement.

Each of us hallucinates a dagger before us, the handle towards our hand (II,i,33)—the dagger of sin and death, which we believe was the instrument for sacrificing God that we could live. It is that dagger that we see before us in every special relationship; that makes it possible for us to survive as an individual at someone else's expense. Our defenses appear to make us safe. Our safety seems attainable through defeating those who are out to get us. Unlike Macbeth, however, we defend our-selves (most of the time, at least) through specialness, and in sophisti-cated, symbolic ways, rather than through out-and-out murder.

Shakespeare's *Macbeth* shows us what life looks like when the veil is stripped away. Similarly, Adolf Hitler showed us our paranoid thought system when the veil of decency was stripped away. This world "is the delusional system of those made mad by guilt" (T-13.in.2:2). The conflicts of the world portray the thought system that underlies it. Remember that it always takes two to have a conflict, and leaders on either side of a conflict—whether called dictators or not—show us the blood-drenched thought system that underlies our very existence. No one in the world is exempt from such a battleground.

"What's done cannot be undone" (V,i,67). The fact that we think we are here is witness to the seeming truth of that statement. It would seem that the murder of God and the destruction of Heaven can no longer be undone. God is finished, and I am proof of that sinful fact. If the life of the body is real, there is no God. If separation and specialness are real, there is no God. As the workbook states: "If pain is real, there is no God" (W-pI.190.3:4).

The message we want to take from this play is that what tormented Macbeth torments all of us, but we cover it over. When we do, it fes-ters within; and what festers within inevitably is projected outward.

Therefore, we will see acted out before us what we secretly believe is our own guilt. We will forever fight against what we perceive to be outside, never realizing it is a defense against looking at what is inside. We feel guilty about what we see in the world because it reminds us of the contents of our minds. Thus we disguise it, saying all is wonderful; not terrible at all. To be sure, some bad things happen, but there is hope, light, love, and peace, too. We convince ourselves the world can yet work. But as long as we delude ourselves into thinking there is hope in the world, we will never discover the true source of our unhappiness: our minds' decision for guilt. We shall return to this later on.

Chapter 2

MACBETH AND THE EGO'S WORLD OF GUILT

We now look in more depth at Macbeth's decisions in the light of the principles of *A Course in Miracles*. We will begin with Macbeth's ambition, *"which o'erleaps itself, and falls on th'other"* (I,vii,27). In *A Course in Miracles* this is known as the principle of *one or the other*, which, as we shall see, is the core of the "authority problem." In Macbeth's case, Duncan is the supreme authority, the King of Scotland, but Macbeth also wants to be king. Obviously, he knows that if this is to happen, the reigning king will have to be deposed, or in some way disposed of. That is exactly what we, as the one Son, understood at the beginning. We wanted to be the reigning authority, but God stood in our way. We thus wrote a script that gives us the role of son, who rises up against his father and kills him in order to get his power for himself. Although Macbeth was a cousin, not Duncan's son, still he was in a filial relationship with him; Macbeth was younger, loved and esteemed by Duncan, who reciprocated that love and esteem. The parallel between Macbeth's script and ours is evident.

Incidentally, this scenario was the basis of Freud's *Totem and Taboo*, in which he explained his theory that civilization came into being when a group of savages rose up against the father, killed and then ate him. In Freud's theory, that ancient patricide became the core of the Oedipus complex. Freud understood well the original story of murder, cannibalism, and usurpation that we act out over and over again.

The Authority Problem

Let us examine a number of passages in which Jesus discusses the authority problem in *A Course in Miracles*, beginning in the text with Chapter 3:

(T-3.VI.7:1) I have spoken of different symptoms, and at that level there is almost endless variation.

Special relationships are about the varied ways—sneaky, subtle, and ingenious—in which we steal from others what we want and leave them for dead, because we now have what we want and they are without it.

(7:2-3) There is, however, only one cause for all of them; the authority problem. This *is* "the root of all evil."

In the Bible, *money* is regarded as the root of all evil. Here, it is the authority problem. If we look at our friend Macbeth, we see how his authority problem, manifest in his craving to be king, became the root cause of the evil that followed. Sin begets guilt; guilt begets fear of punishment; fear of punishment begets the need to defend through further attack. Thus do the guilt-attack and attack-defense cycles begin; cycles that repeat over and over again, interweaving sin, guilt, attack, and defense in a revolving pattern of evil that is the cause of all problems and their perpetuation.

Skip to the middle of sentence 5:

(7:5) ...the authority problem...because it accepts the one inconceivable thought as its premise, can produce only ideas that are inconceivable.

A central concept, repeated frequently in the text and workbook, is that *ideas leave not their source*. This statement from the early part of the text is a version of that principle. The idea of usurpation that gives rise to the authority problem remains in the mind, and can only produce further insane ideas. The authority problem begins with one inconceivable and impossible idea—a thought of inherent nothingness—that I can oppose, attack, and destroy the Will of God, and then substitute my own will for His. In other words, I can be king. I will do what *I* want, not what God tells me to do. That is the prototypical authority problem, which, in this world, translates into everyone's authority problem: "No one is going to tell me what to do. I will do whatever I want."

On the other hand, avoiding the authority problem does not require that one say "Yes" to every request or demand. This is not about the *behavior* of doing or not doing what other people ask or demand. It would be silly not to question authority figures and to always obey them in simplistic, naive fashion, nor would it be particularly helpful to do so. But in so many people there is a flagrant authority problem that manifests as an automatic "No!" regardless of what is asked of them.

They do not even evaluate the information or advice, because their immediate response is to think that if they agree or say "Yes," they are diminished. They want to be the reigning authority, and accepting information or taking advice from someone else amounts to an admission that the other person knows more than they do, so their own authority is threatened. They want to show that they know better; they are the authority. Every adolescent goes through this rebellious stage, which, again, is what we originally did with God.

From that original inconceivable thought arose an inconceivable self and world. All other elements of the ego thought system are derived from the original thought that we did the impossible by defying the Will of God. Arising from that inconceivable premise are the ideas of sin, guilt, fear, attack, murder, specialness, *one or the other*, not to mention the illusion of a cosmos of time and space. All these ideas have never left their source in the mind.

(8:1-2) The issue of authority is really a question of authorship. When you have an authority problem, it is always because you believe you are the author of yourself and project your delusion onto others.

Here is our *in*famous friend, projection: we feel so guilty about what we have done that we project responsibility for it on to others. Every time we are angry or have a judgmental or critical thought, we project our unconscious guilt, exclaiming: "I am *not* the sinner; someone else is." We do not have to approve of what this person does, but getting upset, angry, or losing our peace over it is a red flag telling us that we are projecting on to another our guilt over believing we are our own author—we are God. Because of this guilt, we practically salivate every time there is an opportunity to attack. As a species we love to hurt others: governments other governments; groups other groups; family members other family members. Guilt is why everyone loves to attack whenever the opportunity arises, even if such opportunity is *A Course in Miracles* fantasy.

Remember, too, that *A Course in Miracles* teaches that attack can be anything from a slight twinge of annoyance to intense fury (W-pI.21.2:3-5; M-17.4:3-7). Any degree of loss of peace is the same as any other. In the Course, as with being pregnant, we cannot be just a little bit angry. We are either murderous or loving, and there is no in-between. It is our guilt about our murderousness that is reinforced whenever we experience ourselves as a *self*, which is almost all the time—not to mention, experience ourselves as important, unfairly treated, or special in some way. The very fact that we experience ourselves as separate and independent entities is telling us we have declared ourselves to be the author of our own reality. The guilt over this is so horrendous that we continually have to find fault in others, so that we can project our guilt on to them.

(8:3-4) You then perceive the situation as one in which others are literally fighting you for your authorship. This is the fundamental error of all those who believe they have usurped the power of God.

Whether others are actively attacking or not is totally irrelevant. If you harbor guilt in your mind, you will automatically believe they are threatening you. Even if they are actually behaving in a threatening, attacking manner—even if there are people who are competitive and want to hurt or even kill you—you do not have to take what they do personally. Jesus is talking about *your* perception of others as attacking you, not the projection of their guilt—which has nothing to do with you. You believe you have usurped the power of God; you believe you know what is best; therefore you must believe you are guilty and deserve to pay the price for it. Having denied the thought that you are the original sinner, you are aware only of what others seem to be doing to you. Your ego tells you that if they are doing it to you, they are mean, vicious, unkind, insensitive, unloving, and selfish. Therefore you are justified in putting on the face of innocence and attacking them in self-defense.

(8:5-6) This belief is very frightening to them, but hardly troubles God. He is, however, eager to undo it, not to punish His children, but only because He knows that it makes them unhappy.

The Christian party line is that God wants to punish us, which makes our egos very happy. *A Course in Miracles* helps us to understand that this God sees punishment as the means of undoing our sin; first by punishing Jesus and then punishing us. Thus we embark on a life of sacrifice, hoping God will go easier on us later. Jesus is saying here that God knows nothing about this usurpation of His Will, and He surely does not want to punish us. He does not even know that we left Him, because we have *not* left Him. Our nightmares have no power to change reality.

(8:7) God's creations are given their true Authorship, but you prefer to be anonymous when you choose to separate yourself from your Author.

Everything comes down to that bottom line, which is that we have chosen to separate from the Love of God because we wanted to be the author of ourselves. We do not like the idea that we are the effect and God is the cause. This is the source of everyone's authority problem, whether it is expressed in the form of wielding authority over others, or being afraid to; whether it is expressed in the form of submitting to authority in order to be perceived as a nice person so the authorities will not destroy you, or always rebelling against authority. It does not matter which way you slice it. As long as you believe there are authority issues to contend with, you are secretly reinforcing the belief that you are on your own because you secretly believe you have wrenched authority away from the True Authority. That, again, is the source of all guilt.

Now move to paragraph 10, sentence 3:

(10:3-4) The problem everyone must decide is the fundamental question of authorship. All fear comes ultimately, and sometimes by way of very devious routes, from the denial of Authorship.

The ego's thought system is convoluted and quite complex, the purpose of which is to hide the problem's simplicity—the decision to be autonomous, to be king.

(10:5-7) The offense is never to God, but only to those who deny Him. To deny His Authorship is to deny yourself the reason for your peace, so that you see yourself only in segments. This strange perception *is* the authority problem.

To see oneself "only in segments" is to see oneself as separated. We see our bodies as made up of segments, and certainly we see the Sonship as segmented, too. This comes down to the authority problem, because in Heaven there are no segments—only the One, the Oneness of our true Self as Christ. The very fact we believe we are here—fragmented, separated from those to whom we are compelled to relate in order to have our needs met—is proof we pulled off the impossible. Since we believe we have done so, we cannot avoid the ensuing guilt that devours us with its intensity, and then seeks to devour everyone else. Macbeth's sin is everyone's sin. We want to be king, to be God.

Jean-Paul Sartre, the French existentialist philosopher, is said to have commented astutely: "I am an atheist because if there were a God, I could not bear not to be God!"

In our world we cannot be an authority over everyone, but one of the ways in which we undermine authorities is to be angry at them, which we love to do. Whether public figures or figures in our private lives, we secretly delight in having something on them, because that proves, in our minds, that we have the power, just as it proves that we are separate from them. That is why everyone lives for the next scandal about a public figure. At the ontological beginning, the only way we could justify our revolt against God was to say He was defective: His Love was not enough; He did not give us enough; He did not give us the special attention we wanted. We had to find fault with God so we could justify our separating from Him. If we acknowledged that everything was perfect in Heaven, and if we were perfectly one with our perfect Source, we would never leave, and we would not have our individuality, either. We had to justify going through with the plan of separation, because we had had that first taste of what it means to be an individual and our own authority—authors of ourselves.

To his credit, as we have seen, Macbeth did not attempt to justify what he did. He knew that what he was doing was not justified, which is the nobility of awareness that we, too, should cultivate. If we persist in trying to kill off the authority—still trying to have our specialness needs met—at least we can be aware of what we are doing and be honest enough not to call it by any other name: "I want to rule the universe. That is my goal." At least we can be honest. We do not have to disguise it with spiritual platitudes and fancy ideals. We want to be king, whether it is king of the world, our family, job, profession, circle of friends, or whatever. We want to be the authority and in charge.

If I cannot be king in form, I can be king psychologically by finding fault with others. In that way I acquire the power—at least in my mind—that I crave. If I find fault with an authority—a boss or parent I do not like, for example, and if I get people to agree with me—in effect I am greater than that person and have the power, because I have judged against him and have put him down. That is why we have this strong attraction to criticizing others. Rather than having to combat the authority directly—as, for example, with God, and there is no way we could win that war—we do it in our minds. Or we do it through alliances behind people's backs. Again, that gives us a sense of power and authority.

In our minds we are guilty of the same crime as Macbeth. We still want to kill the king so we can be on top. If you can see this, it will help you understand why, even though you may have studied *A Course in Miracles* for many years, you still find yourself making judgments, becoming angry, intolerant, and impatient. Our judgments give us the power to be God, which is why we luxuriate in being angry and being right. If we could be like Macbeth and at least recognize this is what we are doing, without attempting to justify ourselves by proving another wrong, we are at least opening the door to another Voice. That is the message we can get from this play—a message that poor Macbeth never let himself receive.

We turn now to Chapter 11, paragraph 4 in the section "The 'Dynamics' of the Ego."

(T-11.V.4:1) When we look at the ego, then, we are not considering dynamics but delusions.

Jesus is saying that there are no ego dynamics, because the ego has no power. There is no reality to the ego thought system, which is a series of delusions we made up.

(4:2) You can surely regard a delusional system without fear, for it cannot have any effects if its source is not real.

We demonstrate forgiveness to each other by showing that seeming attacks have had no effect on us. If they have had no effect, then nothing has been done to us. If nothing has been done to us, there is no sin and no cause for guilt. That is how sin is forgiven: We demonstrate that attack has had no effect. That is why it is so important to understand that God knows absolutely nothing about the separation, which was an attack on Him. Our insanity—this hallucination of separation—has had no effect whatsoever on God. He did not give an answer to it; He did nothing because nothing happened. That is the Atonement principle, the paradigm for everything Jesus teaches us about how to behave in the world. God showed us that our seeming sin against Him had no effect. There was no separation. Nothing happened. If nothing happened, there was no cause and no effect. If something has no effect, it is not a cause and therefore does not exist.

Therefore, God's non-response is the perfect expression of forgiveness. If God did indeed respond, it would have meant that something truly had happened. As is explained in *The Song of Prayer*, you cannot genuinely forgive something that you have first perceived and made real; that would be forgiveness-to-destroy (S-2.II). This passage is basically asking us to reflect the Atonement principle with each other. In other words, when tempted to give response—*not* behavioral, but emotionally—think of God and recall His lack of response. And then ask Jesus to help you do the same. To be clear, we are not speaking about behavior, but about the emotional response of having let ourselves be affected by someone else. The peace of God remains beyond the delusional system that is the ego's dream, and all things in it. Without fear, what remains is love's reflection, which is expressed in this world as forgiveness.

(4:3) Fear becomes more obviously inappropriate if you recognize the ego's goal, which is so clearly senseless that any effort on its behalf is necessarily expended on nothing.

The ego's goal is to establish that we are separated and on our own. But separation did not happen, because it could not happen; therefore no response to it makes any sense nor is justified in any way. For that reason, everything in the ego system is senseless. A response of guilt to the belief that we have usurped God's role makes no sense, because we have not usurped God's role. Only in dreams has this occurred, but our dreams have had no effect on truth, which remains as it is.

(4:4-6) The ego's goal is quite explicitly ego autonomy. From the beginning, then, its purpose is to be separate, sufficient unto itself and independent of any power except its own. This is why it is the symbol of separation.

The ego is the symbol of separation, and the reality of the separation seems to be proven by everything in the ego thought system: sin, guilt, fear, attack, suffering, and death. Everything here is a shadow of that thought system, with the same goal: to prove we are autonomous, the core of which is the authority problem.

The thought system of the ego gives rise to guilt. As I have often said, we do not have words or concepts in our language, or in any other language, that can begin to approximate the unbelievable horror of this guilt and the magnitude of our self-hatred. That is why our lives are so filled with pain—inflicting pain on others and experiencing it in ourselves.

The body was *made* to experience both emotional and physical pain, and it derives from the terrifying thought that we deserve to be punished because of what we have done to God. The ego attempts to defend against that guilt by making up a world in which we have endless opportunities to project guilt onto others, magically hoping those people will be found guilty and punished instead of us. This is what gives rise to the *face-of-innocence* syndrome, which involves seeing ourselves as unfairly treated victims. Indeed, we are born into this world as helpless victims of forces beyond our control; we did not choose our genes, parents, environment, or anything else about ourselves. It all just happened to us—at least we so believe.

To summarize, our dream scripts have been written this way to reinforce the idea that pain and suffering are real. Our hope is that others will be held responsible, and therefore they will be punished instead of us. But the inevitable effect of our belief that we have usurped God's role—that we, like Macbeth have killed the king and now stand in his place—is guilt, and that is what gives rise to a world of pain and suffering, which we cannot escape as long as we do not accept responsibility for it. We will now look at a few brief passages that further explain and describe this dynamic.

The Projection of Guilt and Its Consequences

Our first passage comes from "The Unbelievable Belief" in the text, which refers to the ego, of course; specifically to the belief that we are separated from God. It is unbelievable because in truth the separation never happened. In this section Jesus speaks about *projection* without using that term; but he does speak about the effect of the belief in separation, which is our guilt.

(T-7.VIII.3:8) The belief that by seeing it [guilt] outside you have excluded it from within is a complete distortion of the power of extension.

Jesus explains in *A Course in Miracles* that the dynamic of having something in the mind expressed in the body is common both to the Holy Spirit and to the ego. When that process refers to the ego, we call it *projection*: the attempt to get rid of guilt we do not want. When its source is the Holy Spirit, we call it *extension*: the extension of love or forgiveness. Either way, the dynamic of something in the mind perceived to be outside it is the same.

(3:9) That is why those who project are vigilant for their own safety.

Remember Macbeth's statement: *"To be thus is nothing; But to be safely thus...."* (III,i,47). He is not safe, for after what he has done he will never be safe. Macbeth symbolizes that insecurity for all of us. Deep within, we believe we will never be safe because of our sin. We have killed the king and will never remove the stain of blood from our hands, even though we continually try to wash it off by projecting it onto others. As I said earlier, that is why we have such a strong attraction to being angry, making judgments, and finding fault with other people. Projection is how we try to get rid of guilt's stain, but Jesus explains that it does not work:

(3:10) They are afraid that their projections will return and hurt them.

I am afraid of you because what I have projected is the self I believe is a guilty, sinful murderer. That inevitably makes you into the guilty, sinful murderer, and so I will be the object of your murderous thoughts, which of course are really mine: I am the one who attacked you by making you the sinner instead of me.

We all walk this world in mortal fear because we have literally made the world in our own image and likeness, and it is not a very nice one; blood drenched, as in Lady Macbeth's tortured cry, *"...who would have thought the old man to have had so much blood in him?"* (V,i,39). "Duncan's" blood is all over her, and she cannot wash her body clean. In our case, of course, it is not that God literally has blood in Him, but in our tortured, insane minds He was originally filled with the blood of life, which we drained so we could live in His place. The resultant guilt, which is what the blood now represents, permeates our separated self. Every time we take a breath we are not really inhaling oxygen; we are inhaling guilt's blood, because that is what keeps the ego going. We call it oxygen, and we think it is clean, fresh air, but every breath speaks to us of our original sin. Our guilt is so horrific, all we can do is attempt to get rid of it almost as soon as we experience it. Yet, again, once we project it, we must believe it will come back to us. I accuse you of the sin of which I secretly accuse myself. I have made you into my self, and that self is an unrepentant murderer.

To repeat, according to the ego's fourth law of chaos (T-23.II.9), I have what I have taken. I have stolen your innocence, which makes me a thief; and that theft is what I project back onto you. Thus I accuse you of wanting to steal from me, leading to a perception of a world in which I have cause to be afraid. And so we lock our cars and homes, feeling a need to protect our possessions; we have insurance policies and lawyers because everyone is out to get us—from the government on down. We have indeed made up a government that actually *does* want to get us, and we have made up a world where people actually *do* want to get us. We made up a world in which there are viruses and bacteria that want to get us—new ones, in fact, every day. We made up a world of hostility and danger, wherein we are helplessly vulnerable. But this is not unique to our age. It has always been like this. What we are witnessing these days are the veils being lifted, so that the horror of the ego thought system is increasingly revealed. In sum, we must believe people are out to get us, because we secretly believe we have "gotten" them. And so:

(3:11) Believing they have blotted their projections from their own minds, they also believe their projections are trying to creep back in.

We are afraid that our projections will return to hurt us. Instead of me being a murderer, I now stand on the verge of being murdered, unless I do something to protect myself. The world in which we live is not a place of love, light, joy, and peace; it is a world of dog-eat-dog. As we will see, Jesus tells us that it is a world of "kill or be killed" (M-17.7:11); a world in which we are all desperately trying to get rid of the blood of guilt that covers us. As Lady Macbeth could not wash off the blood of her guilt, we cannot do so either.

(3:12) Since the projections have not left their minds, they are forced to engage in constant activity in order not to recognize this.

This "constant activity" is the world we have made: the world we believe in, the world we participate in; the world we strive to make sense of, adjust to, and survive in. In other words, the world consists of the guilt we have tried to get rid of by projecting it onto other people;

but it does not go anywhere. We cannot get rid of it because *ideas leave not their source*. The guilt remains within, so we continue desperately trying to get rid of it, and no sooner do we think we are rid of it, than more comes in, because we never undo the source, which is the thought system that says: "I *have* usurped God's role; I *am still* usurping God's role; I *will always* usurp God's role."

Once Macbeth began killing, he could not stop. He had to protect what he had stolen and killed for. Such defensiveness is what we all do. We are here because we stole life and had to kill for it, at least in our insane imagination, and so we continually kill in self defense, in order to retain the life of our individual self. This is the meaning of special relationships. We continually try to preserve the life we stole from God and the "priceless pearl" of specialness we steal from everyone (T-23.II.11:2), and which we know they are going to try to steal back from us. Each of us makes up everyone else in our own image and likeness, but desperately trying to pretend we are not; rather, we are good, loving, kind, and peace-keeping people.

Once again, to Macbeth's credit, he did not pretend that he was other than what he was and had become. His not pretending is the first step, but he unfortunately does not take any further steps. At least, though, he shows us the first step, which is not to attempt to get rid of that guilty image. Instead of projecting guilt away from yourself, look in the mirror and say: "Yes, this is who I am; this is what I have become." And know that deep down you are choosing it. It is not that this is who you are and you cannot stop it, but rather, you will not stop it. Our insanity is that we like the taste of blood, even as there is a part of us trying to get rid of it, and, as did Lady Macbeth, smear everyone else with it so we will be seen as innocent. But obviously there is a part of us that likes the murder and the blood, because it maintains the illusion of our autonomy, and the price we pay for that illusion is that we must always be on our guard against what the world we made will do to us in return.

Turn now to the Introduction to Chapter 13. Although the ego's use of guilt is discussed earlier in Chapter 5, this chapter provides the first thorough treatment of guilt and, interestingly, is the longest chapter in the text. We shall start at the beginning:

(T-13.in.1:1) If you did not feel guilty you could not attack, for condemnation is the root of attack.

I am guilty because I believe I condemned and attacked God, and the only way I can get rid of my guilt is to project it out and attack other people. Thus, it is not my fault; it is God's fault, Jesus' fault, this Course's fault, my parent's fault, someone's fault—anyone's but my mind's.

(1:2) It is the judgment of one mind by another as unworthy of love and deserving of punishment.

Deep in my mind I believe I am unworthy of love and am the one who deserves punishment; I am the one who killed the king. But through projection I say, "No, the sin is not in me; it is in you. You are unworthy of love—mine and God's—and deserve to be punished." All relationships are based on this projection of trying to punish others because they are not giving us the love, attention, and dedication we believe we deserve. Because we lack Macbeth's brutal honesty, we are unaware of our *wanting* them not to be there for us: we *want* others to betray, abandon, and reject us, and assume no responsibility for it. Thus can we say, "Behold me, brother, at your hand I die" (T-27.I.4:6).

(1:3-4) But herein lies the split. For the mind that judges perceives itself as separate from the mind being judged, believing that by punishing another, it will escape punishment.

This is one of many statements in *A Course in Miracles* that reveal the dynamic and purpose of the ego thought system: I will escape punishment by giving my guilt to you. As long as it remains within me, I know I will be punished; but if I deny the guilt and project it onto you, I will experience you as the guilty one, which means I am innocent because I am literally guilt-*less*. By giving my guilt to you, therefore, you will be punished, following the ego's law that guilt demands punishment. Once again, Macbeth possessed that nobility of awareness that allowed him to know what he was doing—the first step towards letting the ego thought system go.

(1:5) All this is but the delusional attempt of the mind to deny itself, and escape the penalty of denial.

I deny I am this guilty, sinful person—"the home of evil, darkness and sin" (W-pI.93.1:1)—and give the guilt to you in the magical hope I will be free of it. However, as we have seen, what I project remains within my mind. The idea of guilt leaves not its source, much as I desperately attempt to project it from my mind and put it onto you—"the

41

delusional attempt of the mind to deny itself." Thus I continually project guilt, yet continually generate it without knowing it. It is similar to having a fountain inside that never shuts off. I do not like the blood of guilt that circulates, but I do not know its source. I think it comes from you, from the world—bacteria or some other bad thing that is "out there." I do not know it is coming from me, because I magically believe I have split myself off from it and thus made free of the disease of guilt.

(1:6) It is not an attempt to relinquish denial, but to hold onto it.

Projection is not really an attempt to let go of my guilt, but to continually deny it; and by doing that, hold onto it. This is such an insane, perfidious, vicious, and insidious system! So cruel! But we all do it none the less, and nothing has changed since the ego thought system began. As I have been saying repeatedly, *Macbeth* is an instructive literary work because of its searing portrait of the ego thought system. Once you decide against the true King, choosing to destroy Him so you will be king, you unleash a literal hell, which is what the three witches represent. You cannot then help becoming caught up in this hell of cruelty, hatred, and murder, as did Macbeth. I have already mentioned the pointlessness of his decision to have Lady Macduff and her children killed. It advanced his ambitions not at all, for they were of no threat to him. Macbeth kills because he is angry at Macduff. We are no different, for our hatred is without reason and achieves nothing. We therefore need to examine our thoughts of guilt and hate.

(1:7) For it is guilt that has obscured the Father to you, and it is guilt that has driven you insane.

In truth, the king has not been killed. Macbeth not only hallucinated the dagger before him, he hallucinated killing Duncan. It was all a bad dream, but his guilt says otherwise. Remember the lines I mentioned in my introduction:

> Into eternity, where all is one, there crept a tiny, mad idea, at which the Son of God remembered not to laugh. In his forgetting did the thought become a serious idea, and possible of both accomplishment and real effects (T-27.VIII.6:2-3).

By not remembering to laugh at the tiny, mad idea of separating from God—separating from the king and killing him—we took those ideas seriously and they seemed to have real effects. Guilt became real and justified; and a world of murder, hatred, and death inevitably became real to us. Guilt has thus made us totally insane. First, it is insane to believe that we could separate from God; and second, it is insane to feel guilty over what is impossible and never happened. It is then just as insane, if not more so, to believe we can get rid of our guilt and actually feel better by killing everyone else. Remember, "What is not love is murder" (T-23.IV.1:10). Since, as *A Course in Miracles* tells us, there is no love in this world, everything here must be murder. It does not matter whether you pick up a dagger and kill a sleeping king, or you merely have a hateful thought or a thought of criticism or need. They are all equally murderous, as discussed earlier. What makes us insane is the belief this world is reality and that murder will make us happy and bring us peace.

(2:1) The acceptance of guilt into the mind of God's Son was the beginning of the separation, as the acceptance of the Atonement is its end.

Guilt was born the instant we remembered not to laugh at the thought that separation from Totality was possible and desirable. We can therefore say that the acceptance of the Atonement is the acceptance of the unreality of guilt, and that it is never justified, because nothing happened.

(2:2-3) The world you see is the delusional system of those made mad by guilt. Look carefully at this world, and you will realize that this is so.

Now comes Jesus' version of Macbeth's "*Tomorrow and tomorrow and tomorrow*" speech, which concludes with a depiction of life as "*a tale told by an idiot, full of sound and fury, signifying nothing.*" Let us therefore look at our world carefully:

(2:4-11) For this world is the symbol of punishment, and all the laws that seem to govern it are the laws of death. Children are born into it through pain and in pain. Their growth is attended by suffering, and they learn of sorrow and separation and death. Their minds seem to be trapped in their brain, and its powers to decline if their bodies are hurt. They seem to love, yet they desert and are deserted. They appear to lose what they love, perhaps the most insane belief of all. And their bodies wither and gasp and

are laid in the ground, and are no more. Not one of them but has thought that God is cruel.

It is insane to believe we can lose what we love, because love is part of us. How could we lose who we are? We are part of God, but by believing we are separate from Him we have wrenched ourselves from Love. It then appears as if love can indeed be lost.

"Not one of them but has thought that God is cruel." Whether or not we think it consciously, or have a theology that allows for it or not, is totally irrelevant. We *must* think there is a cruel power somewhere, because we are here—and look at the world we live in! Observe how people try to cover the pain that Jesus just described, saying, in effect, "Sometimes things work and I really can be happy here; most people are nice even though bad things do happen." Yet, if you have understood *A Course in Miracles*, you cannot hide from the brutal fact that we are here out of guilt, and the way we try to escape from it is to keep the pain but give the responsibility for it to someone or something else. This passage and Macbeth's speech describe what this world is like, and such a view of the world—indeed, such a world itself—is inevitable once we accept guilt as real. And we know we believe guilt is real because we think we are here. Loving, guiltless people do not come to this world. Jesus never really did, because he knew he was not here. The world perceived a body, but this was not who he knew he was.

Only minds riddled with guilt and overwhelmed with self-hatred believe they are here, thinking they can escape their guilt and God's punishment by coming into this world and hiding in the body. But since the world came from the insane thought system of sin, guilt, fear, hate, and murder, it can be nothing but a shadow of that thought. How could it be anything else? And therefore, how could it be taken seriously?

Look at this shorter rendering of the same idea, from near the end of the text:

(T-31.I.7:4) The certain outcome of the lesson that God's Son is guilty is the world you see.

When Jesus uses the phrase "the world you see" he is not implying that there is actually a world other than what we perceive, another physical world with no guilt in it. He is talking about *the entire world of perception and form—the physical universe*. Throughout *A Course in Miracles* he makes a very clear distinction between the worlds of knowledge and perception. The world of knowledge is non-dualistic— the Mind of God and the Oneness of Heaven; the world of perception is dualistic—a separate and separating illusion.

(7:5-8) It is a world of terror and despair. Nor is there hope of happiness in it. There is no plan for safety you can make that ever will succeed. There is no joy that you can seek for here and hope to find.

As you can see, this is a succinct version of Macbeth's speech, describing the illusory world that guilt made, a world that has become our reality. There is another way of looking at the world, which is to look through the eyes of guiltlessness. The world itself does not change. What changes is our *interpretation* of it, in the sense that we no longer see ourselves as part of the world, and therefore we no longer see ourselves as victimized by what goes on here. However, once we make guilt real, we must walk this earth in "terror and despair," and there is no "hope of happiness in it." When Macbeth took that first step, he knew what he was doing and what would happen. He prayed that he could turn back the clock, but the deed was done and, as Lady Macbeth tragically observed, *"What's done cannot be undone"* (V,i,67). Nothing here will ever work.

Turn now to the teacher's manual, the section called "How Do God's Teachers Deal with Magic Thoughts?" Here we will see the passages I referred to earlier, the closing one borrowed directly from Lady Macbeth's speech.

(M-17.5:3) A magic thought, by its mere presence, acknowledges a separation from God.

In the context of this section, a magic thought is anything done in the world to alleviate pain, bring pleasure, or give hope of happiness. The very fact that I need help from the world to make me happy or alleviate pain is telling me I am living as a body in a world of other bodies—all of which I have made real. This means I have made the thought of separation from God real as well.

(5:4-6) It states, in the clearest form possible, that the mind which believes it has a separate will that can oppose the Will of God, also

believes it can succeed. That this can hardly be a fact is obvious. Yet that it can be believed as fact is equally obvious.

As *A Course in Miracles* explains in many different places, we are free to believe anything we want, but what we believe has no power to make illusions real, or reality into an illusion.

(5:7) And herein lies the birthplace of guilt.

Guilt arises from my belief that I have opposed the Will of God and set up my own will. In other words, I believe it to be a fact that I have killed God and established a world in which I exist as a separated, individual entity.

(5:8) Who usurps the place of God and takes it for himself now has a deadly "enemy."

This passage is a wonderfully succinct summary of the ego's unholy trinity of sin, guilt, and fear. *Sin* tells me I have opposed the Will of God; *guilt* is the horrific feeling that comes from believing in sin; I then project the guilt onto God and consequently *fear* He will attack me in return. God has thus become my "deadly enemy."

(5:9) And he must stand alone in his protection, and make himself a shield to keep him safe from fury that can never be abated, and vengeance that can never be satisfied.

This passage describes what goes on in our minds once we choose to make guilt real. Now we can never be at peace or feel safe. As Macbeth said, *"We have scotcht the snake, not kill'd it"* (III,ii,13). Guilt will always be in our minds. Its venom remains within, and we cannot get rid of it. Hope seems to have died forever.

Now to paragraph 7. The first two sentences talk about why we get angry at other people's magic thoughts—for example, why *Course in Miracles* students become upset when other Course students take an aspirin or go to a doctor, or why anyone gets annoyed at anyone, Course student or not. Jesus explains here that the anger directed towards the actions and thoughts of others have awakened our guilt over the use of magic to satisfy our selfish needs of separation and individuality.

(7:3-4) Each one [each magic thought] **says clearly to your frightened mind, "You have usurped the place of God. Think not He has forgotten."**

As desperately as we may have tried to get rid of our guilt by projecting it onto others, the fact remains that guilt does not leave its source. It remains in our minds, continually generating the fear that God will destroy us. Within the delusional system of the ego in which we believe, God has never forgotten what we have done. It matters not that our sin of separation against God is made up, as are we and our guilt. As long as we believe in the ego's lies, we can never be rid of our fear. Just as Banquo's ghost appeared to Macbeth after his murder, we are always haunted by our guilt and fear: "Think not He has forgotten— His ghost will pursue you and you will never be free."

(7:5-6) Here we have the fear of God most starkly represented. For in that thought has guilt already raised madness to the throne of God Himself.

This is directly related to the second and third laws of chaos (T-23.II), which describe how we craft God in our own image and make Him as insane as we. Later, in the "Laws of Healing" (T-26.VII), Jesus talks about how this insane "God" becomes impatient, loses His Mind, and "splits the world apart" (T-26.VII.7:4). That image directly expresses the ego's fear. We have made God in our image and likeness: a murderer who will stop at nothing to get what he wants. Thus does our guilt make an image of a God that portrays our own insanity and justifies our fear.

(7:7-9) And now there is no hope. Except to kill. Here is salvation now.

There is no way that I can kill God, Who is in my mind. Therefore, I have to make up a world in which I can kill other people, hoping magically that I will be safe. Macbeth depicts that magnificently—he keeps killing because he is never safe. His guilt, like the Energizer Bunny, just keeps on going and going and going.

You may recall that during the arms race in the 50s, 60s, and 70s both the United States and Soviet Union had to build more and more bombs. Forty overkill was not enough. It had to be 100 overkill; even 150 overkill. It was never enough, because deep down we knew we would never be safe—not because of the enemy "out there," but, following the ego's laws, because of the enemy within; an enemy continually generating the guilt that impels us to project as quickly as it arises. And so we see others attacking us as part of an endless and frustrating war in which there can never be a winner. We will never win as long as guilt stays where it is; hidden and therefore uncorrected.

(7:9-11) Here is salvation now. An angry father pursues his guilty son. Kill or be killed, for here alone is choice.

I cannot kill God—I am no match for Him—so I decide to go out of my mind, literally and figuratively. I attempt to leave the mind, which is the locus of the ego's insane and vengeful God, and escape into a world. However, since *ideas leave not their source*, the battleground of *kill or be killed* has simply been transferred from my mind to the world. In this dynamic of *one or the other* it makes no difference whether we murder physically or emotionally; the content remains the same. *A Course in Miracles'* treatment of special relationships focuses on the ways in which we psychologically hurl our brother over a precipice, rip flesh from bone, and send out ravenous dogs of fear to find any trace of sin in others, bringing them back to us for judgment. (See T-24.V.4; T-19.IV-A.12-13.) These are grisly images that Jesus holds up to us, but they show us the true nature of the world; a world we do not want to see.

Now come the lines borrowed from Lady Macbeth's sleepwalking scene:

(7:12) Beyond this there is none, for what was done cannot be done without.

Lady Macbeth said, *"What's done cannot be undone"* (V,i,67). The sin of killing the king and usurping his place can never be undone unless we return to the decision-making part of our minds that chose it. But once we make guilt real, it drives us out of our minds and there is no choice but *kill or be killed*. Guilt is insane and makes us insane. Having been driven from our minds, we actually think we are bodies interacting with bodies that are separate from us. We feel attacked on all fronts: microcosmically by bacteria and viruses, macrocosmically by people. It does not matter whether we are talking about physical or emotional attack; beyond its disparate forms, the content is the same.

The next line is an even clearer reference to Lady Macbeth:

(7:13) The stain of blood can never be removed, and anyone who bears this stain on him must meet with death.

As long as I believe guilt is real—as long as I believe I am separate from my Source—I cannot remove guilt's stain. I magically hope I can get rid of my guilt by smearing its stain on you. Maybe my sense of freedom will last for 15 seconds, but then the cycle of fear begins again. I finally get my special partner to be what I want, give me what I want, love me the way I want, and pay attention to me the way I want—everything is wonderful. Then I awake the next morning and wonder whether he or she will continue to give me what I want. I have no choice: I must continue to project the guilt away from me. It is an unending and totally frustrating situation. "The stain of blood can never be removed, and anyone who bears this stain on him must meet with death." What I believe was done "can never be done without." The only way I can be free is by realizing there was no sin in the first place: the separation never happened. That is why Jesus tells us repeatedly that our sole responsibility is to accept the Atonement for ourselves.

Let us look at two more passages. Turn to Lesson 161 in the workbook. The entire second half of this lesson is wonderfully appropriate in this context, but we will only look at paragraphs 7 and 8, which also describe the world that guilt has made.

Remember, "The world you see is the delusional system of those made mad by guilt" (T-13.in.2:2). Guilt comes from the belief we have murdered God and have usurped His place on the throne, establishing ourselves as creator. Inevitably self-hatred gnaws at us continually, behind which, the ego tells us, is a wrathful God Who hates us even more because of what we have done to Him. The ego then comes to rescue us from this horrendous situation. It assures us that we can get rid of the hate and guilt simply by finding someone upon whose unholy head we can dump it. We need a specific object to hate and to blame, which is why Jesus says earlier in Lesson 161, "Thus were specifics made" (3:1). We made up bodies so that we could perceive sin in others and attack them for it. In paragraph 7 Jesus describes what that attack looks like:

(W-pI.161.7:1-3) Hate is specific. There must be a thing to be attacked. An enemy must be perceived in such a form he can be touched and seen and heard, and ultimately killed.

When we wrote our scripts, we fragmented the Sonship into billions of pieces that afford us wonderful opportunities to find objects to hate. We need a specific body out there, something that takes our attention away from the intolerably painful guilt in our minds. We desperately seek to rid ourselves of the stench of murder, and succeed for brief instants when the projection works. But the odor of evil inevitably rises again.

(7:4) When hatred rests upon a thing, it calls for death as surely as God's Voice proclaims there is no death.

This is the Voice for God that Macbeth screened out, that both he and his wife prayed would never come to disturb what they were doing. Some of you may remember Helen's wonderful poem, "Stranger on the Road" (*The Gifts of God*, p. 103)[4], the setting of which is Helen meeting Jesus along the road after his crucifixion. He was supposed to have been killed, but now he appears. Helen speaks for all of us when, in the first part of the poem, she expresses how disturbing his presence is to her. If Jesus is there, he could not have been killed. If he were not killed, there was no sin; and if there is no sin, there is no separation. No separation, no individual self. Nothing but the Love of God. And so Helen pleads with Jesus: "Do not disturb me now."

In the next stanza of the poem, we hear again an echo of Lady Macbeth: What is done is done forever, and will never be undone; sin and death are real, and they will never change:

> Do not disturb the ending. What is done
> Is done forever. Neither hope nor tears
> Can touch finality....

A few stanzas later:

> Disturb me not,
> I beg of You. I would not see You now.

Clearly, this is another rendering of what we discussed earlier, where both Macbeth and Lady Macbeth tried to block out the light, desperately attempting to screen out the Voice that proclaims there is no death: no sin, no usurpation, no murder, and no blood. There was

---

4. See my audio album based on this poem, "Forgiving Jesus: 'Stranger on the Road,'" listed in the Related Material at the end of Volume IV.

nothing. But if there is nothing—no separation and no sin—I do not exist, and *I want to exist!* The only way I can exist is to kill off all the competition, beginning with God and the one who represents His love for me.

Once again, Macbeth speaks for everyone. He killed Duncan for everyone. Despite his awareness that there is another Voice and a light—a star in his mind that would shine on his *"black and deep desires"* (I,iv,51)— he fought off its presence, as we all do. This is why everyone has so much trouble with this Course, for it would shine a light on our "black and deep desires" and undo everything we believe, everything on which our individual identity rests. Above all, this identity rests on hate, because hate rests on guilt, and guilt rests on our belief that we have separated from God.

(7:4-5) When hatred rests upon a thing, it calls for death as surely as God's Voice proclaims there is no death. Fear is insatiable, consuming everything its eyes behold, seeing itself in everything, compelled to turn upon itself and to destroy.

Seeing myself in you, I am driven to destroy that sinful, guilty image. My fear of my own guilt is insatiable; it compels me to seek sinners "out there," as graphically described in the "Attraction of Guilt" section of "The Obstacles to Peace" (T-19.IV-A.i). The messengers of fear, the "hungry dogs," are kept starving so they will race around madly, filling up their gorges with "things decayed and rotted"—the flesh and bones of corpses who were once the home of sin. That is what we ask fear's messengers to return to us, and that is what we seek as we walk this earth—always trying to find fault; always trying to shift responsibility from ourselves to others; always with an insatiable hunger and deep neediness to have others cover up our guilt, while we secretly try to steal back the innocence we believe they stole from us. In other words, we want the innocence so they keep the guilt.

(8:1) Who sees a brother as a body sees him as fear's symbol.

If I see myself and others as a body, we cannot be joined, and separation is thereby made real: "Minds are joined; bodies are not" (T-18.VI.3:1). I want to see others as bodies, because minds *are* joined and I want to hold on to separation.

(8:2-4) And he will attack, because what he beholds is his own fear external to himself, poised to attack, and howling to unite with him again. Mistake not the intensity of rage projected fear must spawn. It shrieks in wrath, and claws the air in frantic hope it can reach to its maker and devour him.

That is our world. To state this again, nothing here can exist without feeding off something else. That is how the body was made and how it is sustained. It cannot exist without getting energy, food, oxygen, and water from an outside source; and we must constantly combat the terrible experience of loneliness, which reminds us of the original loneliness we experienced when we left Heaven. We therefore continually seek for companionship. Our bodies were made so that they would continually seek for something outside, a topic addressed in that powerful section near the end of the text, "Seek Not Outside Yourself" (T-29.VII).

There is not much we can do about seeking after oxygen, water, and nutrition; but as students of *A Course in Miracles*, we certainly can do something about our special relationships and the neediness that causes us to judge and attack them. We must heed Jesus' strong words: "Mistake not the intensity of rage projected fear must spawn." We always seek to attack, which means we are always seeking to kill in some way. Macbeth provides us with a powerful if not repulsive model of our egos in action.

The last passage I want to read on this theme is from *The Song of Prayer*, from what can be thought of as the pamphlet's coda:

(S-3.IV.5:3) Do not choose amiss, or you will think that it is you who are creator in His place, and He is then no longer Cause but only an effect.

In our delusional thought system we believe we have usurped God's place. We are now First Cause, and have made the true God in our own image. He thinks and acts like *homo sapiens*; the biblical God, of course, being the prime example of this dynamic: He becomes angry, jealous, and murderous; He condemns and "mercifully" practices forgiveness-to-destroy; He embraces specialness, for He loves and hates conditionally; He has good days and bad days; He believes in atonement through sacrifice. Most importantly, He is like us because He believes that sin is real. Thus has God become the ego's effect, no longer the Son's Cause.

(5:4) Now healing is impossible, for He is blamed for your deception and your guilt.

Healing becomes impossible because all our problems are God's fault: God, Jesus, the Holy Spirit, and this Course have lied. They have not really lied, of course, but we *want* them to have lied, and we do not realize that was our wish. We *want* to catch Them in what we believe is a lie, because we think that will release us. If we cannot trust God and Jesus, then we do not have to trust anyone, and that is exactly what we want. We want to trust only ourselves—the ego's illusions instead of the Holy Spirit's truth.

The absolute and utter insanity of this position is that the self we want to trust has already been judged by us to be a betrayer and murderer! That is the very self we try to get rid of through projection, making someone else the faithless one. That is why we dream a dream in which we will be abandoned, betrayed, rejected, abused, and victimized. There is a method in our madness. Again, we want to be hurt so we can point that accusing finger and say: "Behold me, brother, at your hand I die" (T-27.I.4:6).

(5:5) He Who is Love becomes the source of fear, for only fear can now be justified.

As an example, once Macbeth made his fatal decision and took the plunge into the insanity of ambition, his fear was completely justified in his mind, "made mad by guilt." Since it was his dream, his fear became justified by external circumstances as well. He was convinced that people were actually out to get him, which, because of his actions, they were. And they ultimately succeeded.

(5:6) Vengeance is His.

Remember that dreadful statement found in both the Old and New Testaments: "Vengeance is mine. I shall repay, saith the Lord." (See: Dt 32:35; Rm 12:19.)

(5:6-8) Vengeance is His. His great destroyer, death. [God will exact His vengeance through killing.] **And sickness, suffering and**

53

**grievous loss become the lot of everyone on earth, which He aban-
doned to the devil's care, swearing He will deliver it no more.**

This relates to what we read in the Introduction to Chapter 13: "If
this were the real world, God *would* be cruel" (T-13.in.3:1). A world of
sickness, suffering, loss, and death is the lot of everyone on earth,
which God has abandoned to the devil. How could God possibly save
the world or care about it, let alone love it? Look what we did to Him!
That is why this world is so awful, the ego tells us. He did this to us
because of what we did to Him. God wants no part of us. Yet it is insane
to think these ideas of vengeance have anything to do with God, reality,
truth, and love. They have to do *only* with the projection of hatred and
murder in ourselves. And projection lets us think that the hatred and
murder are no longer in us, but in others, including God.

This is as far as we will go in discussing the ego's world—the world
that inevitably resulted from our grandiose fantasies of having usurped
God's role and killing Him off (the authority problem). The world,
then, is the effect of our guilt (the cause). It is such an appalling picture
that we try to disguise it. Like Lady Macbeth, we desperately try to
wash the blood off our hands, but we cannot. We try to sweeten death's
awful stench with perfumes. Indeed, we literally use perfumes and
colognes to disguise the smells of our bodies, which are the symbols of
separation, corruption, and death. We try to make this world nice. We
try to make it happy and peaceful, but there will never be any hope
unless and until we get to the *cause* of the world, which is our decision
for guilt. That is the message of Shakespeare's play: Macbeth's world
of guilt is *our* world. And yet Jesus says to us, "Yes, that is your world,
made by guilt, but there is another world that guiltlessness has made as
well." That world of forgiveness is the subject of the next chapter.

Chapter 3

A RIGHT-MINDED MACBETH

I would now like to speak of the other side—the side Shakespeare omitted. At this point I think we are clear about the horror of what we accuse ourselves of having done, the horror of our guilt and the world that automatically results, the "walking shadow" of the world of guilt. Once the ego's thought system of sin, guilt, and fear is chosen and accepted as reality, there is no way out from within that system. As I quoted earlier, *A Course in Miracles* says that the thought system of the ego is fool-proof; however the next phrase in that quote is: "but it is not God-proof" (T-5.VI.10:6). There is another choice we can make. I have been emphasizing that what is so fascinating about Macbeth— what makes him so attractive as an illustration—is that he was clearly aware of both sides; what we have been referring to as the nobility of awareness. He was clear about what he was choosing and what he was doing; yet once he made that choice, he became so immersed in the thought system of hate, guilt, and murder that he was unable to extricate himself from it. In fact, he did not even try; he just went with it all the way to its inevitable and tragic end.

Jesus tells us in *A Course in Miracles* that when we choose the ego we will eventually experience pain, and the time will come when we will no longer want to tolerate it:

> Tolerance for pain may be high, but it is not without limit. Eventually everyone begins to recognize, however dimly, that there *must* be a better way (T-2.III.3:5-6).

Somehow we know that there must be a better thought system, or a better teacher; there must be a way out of this. That is the choice for guiltlessness, the subject of the next section.

The Choice for Guiltlessness

A Course in Miracles' way of helping us make the choice for guiltlessness instead of guilt is to have us first become aware we have decided for guilt, and have chosen to protect it through projection.

Jesus would have us realize that this decision is related to what we think is a higher purpose: the preservation of our individual self. We want to keep the individual self we believe we stole from God, but we want someone else to pay the price for it; we want to have our ego's cake and eat it, too—and enjoy it! Stated another way, we want to have our specialness without the consequences of guilt. The wish to keep our identity as individuals is what underlies our belief that guilt is real and justified, and so our attacks on others are real and justified as well.

In order to escape the terrible web of guilt, attack, and defense in which we, like Macbeth, are caught, we have to begin the process of looking at what we have chosen, why we have chosen it, and the consequences of having chosen it. The essence of *right-mindedness* is that we look with Jesus not only at our thought system, but at our *decision* for that thought system, understanding that the decision for it is motivated by a desire to remain as God did *not* create us. This is the ego's alternative to Jesus' teaching: "I am as God created me." Indeed, Jesus repeats that statement in varied forms more than 140 times in his Course. This understanding begins as an intellectual concept, but over time it should become an increasingly well-integrated part of ourselves, until it becomes the frame of reference for giving meaning to *all* our experiences in the world. What ultimately brings about that shift is the recognition that we are not the figures in our dreams, but the *dreamers* of the dream.

The dream began with guilt and punishment, a dream of *kill or be killed*. It evolved into a dream of projection, where we sought to make others responsible for what we do not want to accept in ourselves. We thus have to walk with Jesus, retracing our steps along the path of separation, or, as *A Course in Miracles* states, "to be directed up the ladder separation led you down" (T-28.III.1:2). At the bottom rung of the ego's ladder of separation we find ourselves in this world as bodies, accompanied by other bodies with whom we interact. Since this is where we ended up, this is where our journey home must begin.

Asking Jesus for help means asking his help to look at the picture of what we seem to be doing outside, recognizing that it must be a projection of what we believe is inside: "[The world] is the witness to your state of mind, the outside picture of an inward condition" (T-21.in.1:5). The inward condition of guilt leads to an outside picture of guilt: punishment, murder, suffering, and death. The problem of course is that we do not believe it is just an outside *picture*; we believe it is reality. Thus we need a teacher who does not share our thought system; who remains outside it, helping us begin the process of healing by instructing us that what we are experiencing in the world is a projection of what we have first made real in our minds. Thus do we make the shift from wrong-mindedness and its consequences of guilt, suffering, and death, to the right-minded thought system of forgiveness and peace. Without Jesus this shift is impossible. He helps us realize we are never upset for the reasons we think. If, for example, something bothers me about you, it is because there is something bothering me about me that I have chosen not to look at—my guilt. And so I project it onto you. Thus my anger is a red flag telling me there is something amiss in my mind; something rotten in the state of Scotland (to paraphrase *Hamlet* [I,iv,90])—a rottenness in my mind I have chosen, and then chose never to look at again, thereby protecting it from correction.

Jesus thus helps me change my day so it becomes filled with wonderful opportunities for seeing that everything that I have made real in terms of my reaction and experience is the projected effect of a decision I have made in my mind—the cause of what I see and how I react. If I can learn to see that more and more, I will be less and less willing to choose the ego, because I will have seen the pain it is causing me. In Macbeth's case, he was willing to pay that price, and if one looks at the play from the perspective of *A Course in Miracles*, it can be a metaphor for us. Jesus would tell us that if we push him away and choose to screen out the stars of truth, that they not shed their forgiving light on our dark thoughts, we will end up with lives of pain, fear, terror, cruelty, and death.

When we shift our mind's purpose from murder to miracle, the three witches become three angels, for they now reflect back to us our decision for guiltlessness instead of guilt. This is the whole idea: we recognize first that we have three witches in our lives, but also now three angels, and it is our choice which we listen to. And what we choose to listen to is what we will experience. In terms of the play, when the witches appear the implication is that they are summoned; whether directly summoned, as Macbeth does near the end, or, as earlier, reflecting back to him the state of his mind. In our everyday experience, our eyes see what is out there, but what is important is the way we *interpret* what is seen. We will see witches or angels depending on our mind's choice for guilt or innocence, evil or good, fear or love.

57

In summary, therefore, Jesus helps us to understand that what we have made real inside results from an ongoing, moment-to-moment decision to keep the ego thought system alive and well, in order to keep our self alive and well. This entire system is a defense against hearing the Holy Spirit's Voice; that still, small Voice that gently calls us to choose the thought of the Atonement: the separation from God never happened. It is that Voice, the light of the Atonement in our minds, that Macbeth and his wife screened out. They did not want that light to shine, and they did not want to hear that Voice. That is the same Voice that Helen tried to screen out when she said to Jesus in her poem: "Do not disturb me now"—I am happy where I am; I am quite miserable, but I am happy being miserable. I like the reality of death and the pain of this world. Do not disturb me. This is my dream; leave it alone.

We all say that to Jesus: "Do not disturb me now." We say that to *A Course in Miracles*, and we have been saying it right from the beginning, because we are afraid that the thought of Atonement means that *we* never happened. And it *does* mean that. The self that we perceive every morning in the mirror is not who we are. If the separation never happened, then the self that we cherish, feed, and clothe; the body that we live in, and with which we negotiate our way through life—that self never happened because the separation is not real. That is the truth that Macbeth feared, and that each of us fears as well.

Thus Jesus tells us in Chapter 13: "You are not really afraid of crucifixion. Your real terror is of redemption" (T-13.III.1:10-11). We are not really afraid of punishment, pain, and death; we really fear redemption, our acceptance of the Atonement. When we accept the Atonement, we are redeemed from the belief that there was something to be redeemed *from*; we are saved from the belief that there was something to be saved *from*. The Atonement principle states that nothing happened; therefore there is nothing to undo, nothing to heal, nothing to atone for; nothing requiring expiation. There is nothing to do but accept the Atonement for ourselves, which requires only that we look with Jesus at the ego thought system. This means we would look at it *objectively*: without judgment, guilt, or fear. In that looking with the light of Jesus beside us, the darkness in our minds is extinguished. All that remains is the Atonement, and we can say, as did Jesus, "I am the Atonement" (T-1.III.4:1). That is what it means to be in the real world. When we accept the Atonement, we become a manifestation of the principle that says the separation never happened, but to do that requires a willingness to understand that *we* never happened, either. That is why we speak of accepting the Atonement as the last rung of the ladder.

We have to ascend the ladder of Atonement step by step, because our fear is so intense. While we are in the process of ascending, we still maintain a sense of a separated self. But over time, that self feels less victimized, abused, unfairly treated, angry, and fearful, and more peaceful, joyful, and happy. We begin to awaken as we slowly open our eyes to see with Christ's vision that everyone is the same, meaning that no one is different—we have the same ego, the same Holy Spirit, and the same power of mind to choose between the two.

We turn now to the text, the Introduction to Chapter 11:

(T-11.in.3:5) The closer you come to the foundation of the ego's thought system, the darker and more obscure becomes the way.

This is because we become more and more fearful. The foundation of the ego's thought system is the wish to be an autonomous and separate self, and our own creator. We seek to maintain our identities as individual selves no matter what the cost; no matter how many bodies have to be killed; no matter how many times God has to be destroyed and his Son crucified. We are more than willing to pay that price.

Remember what happened with Macbeth shortly after he killed Duncan. Life had become cheap and death meant nothing. Similarly, once we have killed God and stolen life from Him, all that matters is that we hold on to what we have taken. We will actually, or symbolically, kill anyone who stands in our way. Therefore, as we get closer to the foundation on which our selves have been built, we become more frightened of looking. When we are at the outside ring of fear (T-18.IX.3:9)—the lower rungs of the ladder—and all we have to do is to forgive this other person, or let go of some object of specialness, it is not a big deal. But when we begin to get beyond the outer lines of defense to the real issue—the fear of God, the fourth and final obstacle to peace—the fear becomes ever more acute. We are not merely changing from an angry to a happy self, we are beginning to understand that the entire self is an illusion. Then things become "darker and more obscure," because the fear intensifies.

(3:6-8) Yet even the little spark in your mind is enough to lighten it. Bring this light fearlessly with you, and bravely hold it up to

the foundation of the ego's thought system. Be willing to judge it with perfect honesty.

Here Jesus introduces a theme on which he will elaborate in a later section, "The 'Dynamics' of the Ego." We are not going to look at that entire section, but he says the same thing there:

> We are ready to look more closely at the ego's thought system because together we have the lamp that will dispel it, and since you realize you do not want it, you must be ready (T-11.V.1:3).

The "little spark" he refers to in the quote above is the right-minded thought that says there must be a better way; the part of us that says there is something very wrong in our minds. Clearly, looking is not something we can do without his help, and so he is asking us to look at our ego *with him*. Again, what we are looking at is not only the horror of the thought system, not only the charade of blaming everyone else, but the fundamental thought that holds the whole thing in place: we do not want to lose our individual identity. We do not want to disappear into the Heart of God, because God does not recognize us there, and we want to be validated as special individuals. It is the fear of losing our self that is the core of the ego's thought system.

This is also clearly implied in the fifth stage of the development of trust, discussed in the early part of the manual (M-4.I.A). Jesus says that stage can last a very long time. It is the bridge between the fourth and sixth stages, the sixth being the attainment of the real world, and the fourth being the stage where we have learned to forgive and have reached a significant amount of peace. However, it is still the "I" that has learned to forgive; "I" still believe "I" am a self, now a forgiving self. The fifth stage, the referent here, is when we begin more fully to understand what is involved in accepting the Atonement. This is not a stage one should rush into. If we do not go slowly, one step at a time, we will be thrown into a panic, and then we would be tempted to defend against the panic by thinking that everything is fine and we are already in the real world, filled with its light and peace. That is why Jesus reassures us:

> Fear not that you will be abruptly lifted up and hurled into reality. Time is kind, and if you use it on behalf of reality, it will keep gentle pace with you in your transition (T-16.VI.8:1-2).

We will not be jumping from nightmares to awakening, he tells us; we will first have gentle and happy dreams of forgiveness:

> You will first dream of peace, and then awaken to it. Your first exchange of what you made for what you want is the exchange of nightmares for the happy dreams of love (T-13.VII.9:1-2).

> Vision is the means by which the Holy Spirit translates your nightmares into happy dreams... (T-20.VIII.10:4).

We go slowly, and we begin the process by gradually disidentifying from the body, and identifying more and more with the mind; identifying less with the self who is a figure in the dream, and more with the self that is the dreamer of the dream.

Within the illusion, the self of the split mind is the decision maker; everything else is a defense against this understanding. This self is not sinful or sinless; it is not a body, nor is it special. It is simply the self that can choose to be sinful or sinless, mind or body. Actually, we never cease to be a decision maker. The body was made to keep us from realizing that we are a mind, and thus hide our decision-making power from us. The purpose of *A Course in Miracles* is to help us leave that state of mind*less*ness and return to the state of mind*ful*ness. This is Jesus' point, and so he says:

(3:8-9) Be willing to judge it with perfect honesty. Open the dark cornerstone of terror on which it rests, and bring it out into the light.

At the end of the text Jesus talks about the "shrouded vaults" in our minds that have been closed off by guilt, and then sealed by the world and body (T-31.V.6:6)—the ego's double shield of oblivion (W-pI.136.5:2)—so that we never return to the dark cornerstone of the ego thought system. Jesus is asking us to let him help us get back to that cornerstone. "Let us together open it up and look at the foundation of your terror, and in the light it will be seen as nothing," as we now read:

(3:10) There you will see that it rested on meaninglessness, and that everything of which you have been afraid was based on nothing.

Macbeth's tale is *"full of sound and fury, signifying nothing"* (V,v,26). It is all nothing. But to Macbeth it is a *real* nothing. To Jesus, it is a nothing that truly is nothing: the body and its life are a projected illusion defending against the Everything.

(4:1) My brother, you are part of God and part of me.

That rules us out as an individual self, separated from Christ and our Creator.

(4:2) When you have at last looked at the ego's foundation without shrinking you will also have looked upon ours.

That is the foundation of the Atonement, which has been covered over by the ego's foundation of illusions of reality.

(4:3-8) I come to you from our Father to offer you everything again. Do not refuse it in order to keep a dark cornerstone hidden, for its protection will not save you. I give you the lamp and I will go with you. You will not take this journey alone. I will lead you to your true Father, Who hath need of you, as I have. Will you not answer the call of love with joy?

This is the call that Macbeth and Lady Macbeth screened out. It is the call that all of us have tried to screen out, and that is why we are here. We deceive ourselves if we think we are different from Macbeth and his wife. We are in the world because we believe we are murderers. We have the illusion that our body sleeps, but just as Macbeth heard a voice cry *"sleep no more!...Macbeth shall sleep no more!"* (II,ii,40), our minds are always awake; awake with guilt so that we have no true rest and peace. Yet hidden behind our guilt is the thought of the Atonement. However, we cannot reach the peace it offers us unless we first go through the ego thought system, which begins with the acknowledgment we are killers. Early in the text Jesus says, "Rest does not come from sleeping but from waking" (T-5.II.10:4), and we awaken with Jesus as we forgive.

We return now to "The 'Dynamics' of the Ego."

(T-11.V.10:1) Your recognition that whatever seems to separate you from God is only fear, regardless of the form it takes and quite apart from how the ego wants you to experience it, is therefore the basic ego threat.

What separates us from God is simply our fear. It is not the world or body, but our *thought system* that separates us from God—the fact the ego never wants us to know. It certainly wants us to know fear, but fear of the world—of being hurt, not having enough money, getting older; all things associated with the body. But the ego keeps from our awareness that our unhappiness is due solely to *the thought system of fear in our minds*. If we knew that, and knew our belief in the ego is a defense against the thought system of love that is also in our minds, we would make the change at once. Thus the purpose of the world: to keep us from making that change.

(10:2-3) Its dream of autonomy is shaken to its foundation by this awareness. For though you may countenance a false idea of independence, you will not accept the cost of fear if you recognize it.

"*If* you recognize it"—that is the key phrase. *If* we really knew what we were doing, we would stop doing it. *If* we truly recognized we are maintaining separation each and every time we held a thought of specialness—hurt, anger, attachment—and this separation was the cause of our pain, we would stop choosing those thoughts. This recognition must be more than intellectual, and what prevents us from attaining it on the experiential level is the thought that if we allow ourselves truly to recognize that the source of fear is in our minds and that we can choose against it, we will lose our identity. And that is true! The ego's dream of autonomy—our very life—is shaken to its foundation by that awareness. I believe I am an autonomous individual, and this special, important self is threatened by the awareness I am a mind, and that fear is the result of my own decision. It is essential we understand this, because it will help us become kinder and gentler with ourselves, as well as with others.

This is not a difficult Course in terms of what it asks of us. It is difficult only when we cling to that self-identity that is threatened by honest self-examination and awareness, and therefore does not want to learn what this Course teaches. To learn *A Course in Miracles* does mean the end of *that* self: "Its dream of autonomy is shaken to its foundation by this awareness."

We skip to paragraph 11:

(T-11.V.11:1) If the ego's goal of autonomy could be accomplished God's purpose could be defeated, and this is impossible.

It is *one or the other*, and the Atonement principle states that God's purpose *cannot* be defeated; therefore ego autonomy is impossible. God's purpose, Self, and Will are perfect Oneness, in which there is no individual autonomy. It is impossible to be separated from Who and What we are.

While it is important to understand where *A Course in Miracles* is leading us, at the same we must pay attention to our daily experiences in the world. We do not take one giant leap from the ladder's bottom to its top, nor do we awaken instantly from nightmares to reality. For a while we maintain our sense of self, but it shifts from an angry, vicious self to a forgiving one. Gradually, we begin to shift our center of orientation from the body to the thought that sustains the body. As we choose Jesus as our teacher, we step back with him and watch our egos in action—that is the meaning of asking him for help. We watch the ego plot, manipulate, luxuriate in pain, seek to harm in order to get what it wants, be selfish and self-centered. And then we smile. As we do this day in and day out, we become aware that the part that is watching is not the self being watched. The observer is the decision maker. Thus, looking with Jesus helps us shift our identification from the figure in the dream to the dreamer of the dream.

(11:2) Only by learning what fear is can you finally learn to distinguish the possible from the impossible and the false from the true.

We recognize that fear is not caused by something external. As Lesson 5 teaches: "I am never upset for the reason I think" (W-pI.5). Therefore I am never angry for the reason I think; nor anxious nor fearful. Recognizing this is what helps us distinguish the false from the true, the wrong from the right mind.

(11:3-4) According to the ego's teaching, *its* goal can be accomplished and God's purpose can *not*. According to the Holy Spirit's teaching, *only* God's purpose can be accomplished, and it is accomplished already.

We are beginning to understand there are two thought systems. The ego thought system we have chosen brings us pain and does not make us happy. The right-minded thought system leads us out of pain. The Holy Spirit will take us through the circle of fear, as is discussed in "The Two Worlds," but God is on the other side (T-18.IX.3:7-9). It is just about impossible to avoid dealing with the fear of losing one's self, and our specialness is the ego's means of keeping us from ever realizing the source of that fear—the mind's decision to be separate.

Now turn to one final section, "The Decision for Guiltlessness" (T-14.III), beginning with paragraph 4.

(T-14.III.4) Each day, each hour and minute, even each second, you are deciding between the crucifixion and the resurrection; between the ego and the Holy Spirit. The ego is the choice for guilt; the Holy Spirit the choice for guiltlessness. The power of decision is all that is yours. What you can decide between is fixed, because there are no alternatives except truth and illusion. And there is no overlap between them, because they are opposites which cannot be reconciled and cannot both be true. You are guilty or guiltless, bound or free, unhappy or happy.

This is a crystal-clear statement about the nature of the split mind: the ego's wrong mind of guilt and crucifixion; the Holy Spirit's right mind of guiltlessness and resurrection; and, implicitly, the part of our minds that chooses—the "you" to whom Jesus speaks. As Jesus explains in "Rules for Decision" (T-30.I), our choices are fixed. The split mind offers only two options, and that is a given. It is important we become completely clear about these two choices, and how we continue to decide between them—over and over—from the time we awake to the time we go to bed, and throughout the night in our dreams. We always choose one or the other. Any time we are not at peace, are upset in any way, we must be able to link the *effect*—how we feel—to the *cause*—the decision in our minds. We can choose only between these two. In a sense, the goal of *A Course in Miracles* is summarized in this one paragraph: to have us reach that state of mindfulness in which the power to choose has been restored to our awareness.

(5:1-5) The miracle teaches you that you have chosen guiltlessness, freedom and joy. It is not a cause, but an effect. It is the natural result of choosing right, attesting to your happiness that comes from choosing to be free of guilt. Everyone you offer healing to returns it. Everyone you attack keeps it and cherishes it by holding it against you.

This is true because the mind of God's Son is one. Whatever I give to you—whether guilt or forgiveness—I reinforce in myself. We can truly give only to ourselves.

(5:6) Whether he does this or does it not will make no difference; you will think he does.

This is an extremely important statement. It does not matter whether people really are out to get you, or you are just imagining that they are. All that is important is what you are thinking in your mind. The tragic drama of *Macbeth* shows us what happens to a mind that becomes obsessed with guilt. Because of its immensity, Macbeth continually perceived people as his enemies; and in the end, people *were* his enemies because he alienated them and tried to kill as many as he could. The guilt was in his mind whether they were out to get him or not. Once you believe you are a sinner—which we all must believe, otherwise we would not be here—the dynamic of projection automatically requires that you believe people are going to do to you what you secretly believe you did to them.

(5:7-9) It is impossible to offer what you do not want without this penalty. The cost of giving *is* receiving. Either it is a penalty from which you suffer, or the happy purchase of a treasure to hold dear.

If I offer you forgiveness, that is what I will receive; that is what I will be reminded of in myself. If I offer you guilt through attack, then guilt is what I will receive, both because I have attacked you, which reinforces my guilt, and also because I *have* to attack. That tells me I am guilty, because otherwise I would not feel I have to attack. The guilt is continually being reinforced—continually regenerating, being projected, being the source of our attacking, attacking, and attacking. Yet all this can be undone through forgiveness, the gift of the Holy Spirit that reflects the treasure of God.

(6:1) No penalty is ever asked of God's Son except by himself and of himself.

God does not ask a penalty of us. It is not His Will that we suffer and sacrifice, be martyred or crucified. Neither can anyone else exact a penalty from us. My body might be punished and sacrificed, but *I* cannot be, because I am *not* a body. If I believe I am guilty, I will believe others are punishing and mistreating me. But if I do not come from the premise of my guilt, but rather from the premise of innocence, regardless of what others do I will recognize it has nothing to do with me. That is the key element in learning to forgive: "What does this have to do with me?"

If I have made the decision for guilt by wanting to kill off God, usurp His place, and be my own creator and authority, I must believe that others will do the same thing to me. Whether or not they act it out is irrelevant. If, on the other hand, I recognize that all this is made up and nothing has happened to separate me from the Love of God—nothing has happened to split my mind and separate me from the love of Jesus—I will not be affected by what other people do. I will know it has nothing to do with me, no matter what it is they do. My mind remains innocent, and so I am beyond all penalty since I am beyond all guilt.

My guiltlessness frees me to look upon others without projection, and see everything they do as either an expression of love or a call for it. Either way, my response will be loving. I do not even have to know the difference between someone's expressing love or calling for it. If I am coming from that quiet place of love within myself, nothing anyone does or says will have any effect on me. If it *does* have an effect—for instance, if a news broadcast upsets me—it can only be because I first made the choice not to be peaceful, by disregarding the voice of peace within. The act of pushing peace away stirs the memory of my original act of pushing peace away, and my horrendous guilt leaves me no option but to deny responsibility, project it out, and blame my distress on whatever seems to have happened or is happening outside. The truth is that our loss of peace is never a result of anything external. No one else can ever punish us or deprive us of peace. It is only our mistaken choice that can bring that about.

(6:2) Every chance given him to heal is another opportunity to replace darkness with light and fear with love.

Every moment throughout the day—each day, hour, minute, and second—I can make that choice, regardless of what is going on around me. I could have been in Auschwitz, or any other death camp, and it would have had no effect on my inner peace. It would certainly have had an effect on my body, but not on my mind, as long as I chose the Holy Spirit as my Teacher instead of the ego.

(6:3) If he refuses it he binds himself to darkness, because he did not choose to free his brother and enter light with him.

That is exactly what Macbeth did. He was very clear that he was refusing the light and binding himself to darkness, to a darkened world of murder, hatred, cruelty, and guilt. He did not free his brother and enter the light with him. He did not see Duncan as one with him, but rather as a competitor. This made the king, and everyone who followed, a victim of the principle of *one or the other.* As long as we identify with a body, that same sequence is inevitable. As long as we identify with a separate self, it is impossible not to see ourselves as vulnerable, living in a highly threatening world where everyone is poised to attack. That is because we came into this world by virtue of our attack on God. It is not as important to understand the metaphysics of *A Course in Miracles* as it is to understand that our upset has nothing to do with any external threat.

(6:4) By giving power to nothing, he throws away the joyous opportunity to learn that nothing has no power.

"Giving power to nothing" is the effect of guilt, which gives power to the nothingness inherent in the decision to kill God and usurp His authority. By giving power to guilt, we throw away the joyous opportunity of learning that the separation never happened, and therefore has no power to affect us in any way. Guilt is the problem, for it infuses the illusory thought of sin with reality, which is how the phenomenal world of guilt becomes manifest.

(6:5) And by not dispelling darkness, he became afraid of darkness and of light.

We become afraid of the darkness of murder in the world because we are afraid of the darkness of murder in ourselves. The dynamic of fear and its consequences are nothing but defenses against the light, in whose presence our individual selves would disappear.

(6:6-7) The joy of learning that darkness has no power over the Son of God is the happy lesson the Holy Spirit teaches, and would have you teach with Him. It is His joy to teach it, as it will be yours.

Darkness has no power over the Son of God. That is the bottom line of Jesus' message to us. Nothing we or anyone else does—no matter how hateful—can affect our true Self. But if we feel guilty about our hateful thoughts, or if we react to other people's hateful thoughts, thereby making them real, we are affirming that the world of darkness is fact and the world of light illusion. We are, in essence, saying that our egos have power over God. Guilt gives that power to the ego, for it warns us not to laugh at the tiny, mad idea. It is serious! And not only is it serious, it has very real and serious effects. Believing that, we make up a world that does indeed seem very serious. And to bodies it is serious indeed. As the text says: "Are thoughts, then, dangerous? To bodies, yes!" (T-21.VIII.1:1-2).

However, if I know I am not a body, and that my self is a figure in a dream that is occurring in my mind, what happens in the world can have no effect on me. Obviously, the daily practice of that principle is difficult, but the world's purpose is to give power to darkness, and our choosing to believe in guilt reinforces the seeming reality of the darkness. Again—*guilt is the problem.* It says the separation has happened and is sinful; so horrible in fact that we deserve to be punished by death. The practical application of this understanding comes in the daily recognition that we have the power of choice. Nothing "out there" can *make* us upset or happy, and we need to observe how we are constantly giving away the power to choose. We need simply look at our decision without guilt and without judgment.

(7) The way to teach this simple lesson is merely this: Guiltlessness is invulnerability. Therefore, make your invulnerability manifest to everyone. Teach him that, whatever he may try to do to you, your perfect freedom from the belief that you can be harmed shows him that he is guiltless. He can do nothing that can hurt you, and by refusing to allow him to think he can, you teach him that the Atonement, which you have accepted for yourself, is also his. There is nothing to forgive. No one can hurt the Son of God. His guilt is wholly without cause, and being without cause, cannot exist.

In order to apply this principle—*A Course in Miracles'* version of "turning the other cheek"—you must realize how tempting it is to show others how they *have* hurt you; how you *do* want to demonstrate their guilt by showing your vulnerability to their attack. That honesty—the nobility of awareness—is how you bring the message of a wonderful passage like this into your daily life. Humbly allow yourself to be in touch with how much you *want* to make others guilty by showing them how unhappy and miserable you are, how your failure is the effect of their sinful cause. For example: "I will show my mother and father what miserable parents they were. Look at what a mess I am, and it is all their fault!" If those thoughts are lurking in your mind, then you surely do not *want* to be happy or successful, because if you are, then how can you prove *they* are guilty?

If the name of the game is to make the other person guilty—and that *is* the name of the ego's game—our vulnerability is the damning accusation of another that says, "Behold me, brother, at your hands I suffer, I'm imperfect, and I'm miserably unhappy. Ultimately, at your hands I get sick and die." Try to see how wedded you have become to that way of thinking, the ego's reigning principle: "*You* did this to me!"

Jesus is teaching you that not only is that accusation of guilt an attempt to hurt someone else, it clearly hurts *you*. Not only does it reinforce someone else's ego identification, it reinforces your own. The fact of the matter is that the Son of God cannot be hurt. Thus Jesus would have you say to your brother: "There is nothing to forgive because you have not done anything to me. You may have done something to my body, but the Love of God within my mind is totally unaffected by anything you have done."

Remember, we should take God as our model. His Love knows nothing about the separation, for it had no effect. God demonstrates that the separation never happened by the fact that He cannot see it and knows nothing about it. That becomes a model for us to reflect in our own lives. We need to demonstrate to others that their seeming sins have had no effect on us. But we have to be honest and vigilant within ourselves to see how much we *want* to suffer; how exquisite the pain is. If we scratch beneath the surface, we will become embarrassingly aware of how exquisite it feels to be in pain—especially emotional pain—and then be able to blame others for it. We love to make people feel guiltily responsible for how we feel, because that is how we keep the separation we stole, yet have someone else be held accountable and be punished for it.

Skip now to paragraph 15.

(15:1-2) Seek not to appraise the worth of God's Son whom He created holy, for to do so is to evaluate his Father and judge

against Him. And you *will* feel guilty for this imagined crime, which no one in this world or Heaven could possibly commit.

Whenever we attempt to judge someone, we are recalling our original judgment against God for withholding special love from us, and then our judgment against ourselves for having retaliated for His perceived rejection of us. From that point on we have continued to live lives of judgment, and can never avoid the guilt over our sin.

(15:3) The Holy Spirit teaches only that the "sin" of self-replacement on the throne of God is not a source of guilt.

If only Macbeth had heard that! If only we could hear it!

(15:4-8) What cannot happen can have no effects to fear. Be quiet in your faith in Him Who loves you, and would lead you out of insanity. Madness may be your choice, but not your reality. Never forget the Love of God, Who has remembered you. For it is quite impossible that He could ever let His Son drop from the loving Mind wherein he was created, and where his abode was fixed in perfect peace forever.

This is a lovely statement of the Atonement principle. "Nothing happened. There is nothing to atone for; there is nothing to feel guilty about. You never left your Father's house." That is what the still, small Voice always whispers to us. The sin of usurping God's place—murder, judgment, and specialness—is not a source of guilt. It is our *belief* in sin that is the source of guilt. Guilt does not come from the "act" of sin, or even from the thought of sin. It comes from our taking that thought seriously and remembering not to laugh at the tiny, mad idea of wanting to be separate from God.

Therefore, we need watch ourselves constantly making judgments, attempting to gain specialness, harboring thoughts of manipulation, seduction, and hatred—all the terrible things we live by in this world. We need to realize why we are doing this, and where these thoughts are coming from. They arise not because we are sinful, but because we are fearful. We are merely seeking to protect our little self from the "onslaught" of love. That is not something for which we should be punished, but gently corrected by looking without judgment at our ego's madness. This allows us to accept the Atonement in the peace by and from which it was given us.

Turn now to paragraph 17, which reflects the principle that leads us from the decision for guilt to the decision for guiltlessness. Remember, the decision for guilt is based on the belief in separation: I am guilty because I committed the self-centered, selfish sin of separating from God, thereby killing Him off. It was *one or the other*, and in order for me to have what I wanted, God had to suffer and pay the price of my freedom. As with Macbeth, my ambition *"o'erleaps itself, and falls on th'other"* (I,vii,27). Our ambition to be king—to be on our own—means we have to destroy someone else; someone has to be sacrificed and killed for us to live. The answer to the belief in sin, murder, and guilt is the Oneness that cannot be compromised. No matter how much we may dream of being separate and on our own, our dreams do not affect reality. The reflection in this world of that perfect state of Oneness is what will eventually lead us back home. That is the essence of Jesus' message in this wonderful paragraph:

(17:1) How gracious it is to decide all things through Him Whose equal Love is given equally to all alike!

Notice that the concept of equality is mentioned three times in one clause of this sentence: *"equal* Love is given *equally* to *all* alike." We must begin where we are—at the bottom of the ego's ladder of separation. We must recognize how we do *not* believe that everyone is equal. We have special love and special hate partners. We believe there are victims and victimizers; people who are innocent and those who are guilty; the good who deserve to be saved, and the bad who deserve to be punished—evil, sinful people who differ from the rest of us. Perceiving differences is the way we live our lives. Thus we have good and bad parents; good and bad siblings; good and bad days; young and old bodies. We are always making distinctions, believing we are separate and different. None of this reflects the Love of God, in Whom we are all the same. God's Love is given to all, and in equal measure to all.

(17:2) He leaves you no one outside you.

We are all the same. That is the bottom line in the daily practice of *A Course in Miracles,* reflecting the decision from guilt to guiltlessness. Guilt separates and sees differences. Guiltlessness recognizes there is no separation and we are not different. Surely we are different in *form*—within the illusion. But we are the same on the level of mind. Once again, we have the same ego—the hate-filled, cruel, murderous self that Macbeth exhibited; the same right-minded love on which Macbeth turned his back; and the same power to choose between them. No one here is exempt from this structure of the mind. That is another way of understanding the above statement: "He leaves...no one outside you." We are all the same.

(17:3-4) And so He gives you what is yours, because your Father would have you share it with Him. In everything be led by Him, and do not reconsider.

In *everything*—every hour, minute, and second of your life—you make a choice. Every time you see yourself tempted to become angry or upset, you can choose to go within and ask for help. That marks the end of guilt. When you do not make that choice, you express your belief that separation is real, and that there are causes outside yourself that are responsible for your pain, misery, and unhappiness—someone or something out there has done this to you! When you catch yourself thinking that way, remember that you are in this world and having this dream to enable you to say that you are not responsible for your current miserable state: a virus made you sick; the stock market made you sick; or the weather, a public figure, or family member. Anything or anyone but *you*! Thus does Jesus plead with us: "Do not reconsider your choice for me, but always come to me for help."

(17:5-6) Trust Him to answer quickly, surely, and with Love for everyone who will be touched in any way by the decision. And everyone will be.

"For *everyone*." If I choose guilt, I am reinforcing that decision in everyone throughout the Sonship. If I choose guiltlessness, I am reinforcing that decision in everyone throughout the Sonship—because *minds are joined*. Forgiveness is all-inclusive; otherwise it is not true forgiveness.

(17:7-8) Would you take unto yourself the sole responsibility for deciding what can bring only good to everyone? Would you know this?

Obviously our answer to that question must be "No." But there is Someone within us Who does know, and the way He helps us learn that everyone is the same is by encouraging us to bring to Him *all* our wishes to be separate and special; *all* our temptations to see ourselves as unfairly treated.

Thus you are asked—day in and day out—to monitor your mind and be vigilant for those moments when you are tempted to make something unreal and illusory into something serious. You make it serious by giving it the power to affect you. *You* give it the power to take away the love and the peace of God within you. Nothing in the world has that power unless you give it to it, which means that all the power in this world is yours—not the power to do things on the level of the body, but to do things on the level of the *mind*, which is the only level that matters within the dream.

Following the previously quoted passage about forgetting to laugh at the tiny, mad idea, we read the following answer to the "serious" problem that guilt has wrought:

> Together, we can laugh them both away, and understand that time cannot intrude upon eternity. It is a joke to think that time can come to circumvent eternity, which *means* there is no time (T-27.VIII.6:4-5).

Once again, Jesus appeals to us to ask him for help, that we look through his eyes at the world and not see it as a hostile, threatening place in which we are vulnerable and at the mercy of forces beyond our control. Rather, his vision teaches us this world is but a classroom in which we learn there is nothing out there that can take away the experience of his love and the presence of his peace: "Not one note in Heaven's song was missed" (T-26.V.5:4). Nothing happened to disrupt Heaven's song of love and peace.

We are not asked to accept the totality of the Atonement principle, because that would mean the end of everything, including ourselves, and this would merely induce a panic. But we are asked to remember that principle every time we are tempted to perceive ourselves unfairly treated and victims of forces beyond our control. In those instants we sing the ego's song of guilt, making Macbeth's world our world, thus making our lives meaningless and without hope. When we turn to Jesus or the Holy Spirit for help—the decision for guiltlessness—everything is different. The outer world does not necessarily change, but how we *experience* it is dramatically different. In the end it is our experience that is everything, because there is no outer world. Our right-minded experience corrects and undoes our wrong-minded experience, and eventually both disappear. All that remains is the Love of God and our true Self.

CONCLUSION

SONG OF INNOCENCE

I would like to close by reading a modified version of Macbeth's speech. I have called Shakespeare's original the "Song of Guilt." With apologies to the Bard I have rewritten Macbeth's soliloquy so that it becomes the "Song of Innocence." Perhaps some readers will remember my discussion of two parallel poems of William Blake in my workshop entitled "The Quality of Mercy," which was based on Shakespeare's *The Merchant of Venice*. Blake gave both wrong-minded and right-minded views in his collections: "The Songs of Experience" and "The Songs of Innocence." The former reflected the ego's world of guilt and hatred, while the latter reflected Who we truly are. Blake's poems were thus the inspiration for reworking Macbeth's speech so that it could represent the right-minded ending of the play.

Just as in *A Course in Miracles* we see Jesus take the ego's nightmare myth and recast it, keeping its shape but giving it a different purpose, one can thus do the same with the ego's song of guilt, turning it into something else. This "Song of Innocence" is the same as Macbeth's "Song of Guilt," but with the ego's words replaced by the Holy Spirit's. Our doing so reflects the shift wherein our lives are no longer a tangled succession of meaningless tomorrows, leading from nothing to nothing, but classrooms of forgiveness in which we are gently led along the path of love and lilies—from guilt to innocence—which opens into Everything:

> Tomorrow, and tomorrow, and tomorrow,
> Walks in this guiltless pace from day to day,
> To the last syllable of recorded time;
> And all our yesterdays have lighted lamps
> The way to eternal life. Out, out, brief candle!
> Life's but reflected light, a happy learner
> That kindly dreams his hour upon the stage
> And then is heard no more: it is a tale
> Told by Jesus, full of love and lilies,
> Signifying Everything.

APPENDIX

SONG OF GUILT

To-morrow, and to-morrow, and to-morrow,
Creeps in this petty pace from day to day,
To the last syllable of recorded time;
And all our yesterdays have lighted fools
The way to dusty death. Out, out, brief candle!
Life's but a walking shadow, a poor player
That struts and frets his hour upon the stage
And then is heard no more: it is a tale
Told by an idiot, full of sound and fury,
Signifying nothing.

Macbeth (V,v,18)

SONG OF INNOCENCE

Tomorrow, and tomorrow, and tomorrow,
Walks in this guiltless pace from day to day,
To the last syllable of recorded time;
And all our yesterdays have lighted lamps
The way to eternal life. Out, out, brief candle!
Life's but reflected light, a happy learner
That kindly dreams his hour upon the stage
And then is heard no more: it is a tale
Told by Jesus, full of love and lilies,
Signifying Everything.

(with apologies to Shakespeare)

INDEX OF REFERENCES TO *A COURSE IN MIRACLES*

INDEX